Acknowledgements

Stephanie Mathivet, Curriculum and Standards Manager,

Pre-school Learning Alliance

Contents

Introduction

This publication provides an introduction to safeguarding children for practitioners working in early years settings. It is framed within the government guidelines for safeguarding children as well as the policy context of the Pre-school Learning Alliance.

Working Together to Safeguard Children (HMG 2010) makes clear the difference between safeguarding and child protection. Safeguarding and promoting the welfare of children is defined as:

■ Protecting children from maltreatment.

■ Preventing impairment of children's health or development.

■ Ensuring children are growing up in circumstances consistent with the provision of safe and effective care.

■ Enabling those children to have optimum life chances and to enter adulthood successfully.

Child protection is defined as:

■ Being an element of safeguarding and promoting welfare.

■ Activity that is undertaken to protect specific children who are suffering or are likely to suffer significant harm.

The idea is that if agencies and individuals work pro-actively to safeguard all children, it will reduce the number of individual children who will be in need of protection.

Safeguarding and promoting children's welfare and protecting children depends on adhering to four essential dos and don'ts:

■ **Do** put children's welfare as your first consideration.

■ **Do** record anything which gives cause for concern.

■ **Don't** feel that it would harm the relationship with the family if you took your concerns to children's social care.

■ **Don't** act alone or think you can manage a situation without referring. You can't!

Differences in values and traditions

In any society there are differences in the way in which people bring up their children; views on what is the 'right' or 'best' way change as society changes, so views on child rearing are not static. In culturally diverse societies these differences in values and traditions add further complexity. Children from many different cultures and traditions can grow up to achieve well-being in all aspects of their lives. So there is no absolute right or wrong way to raise children. Practitioners must therefore be aware of their own values and judgments and how these in turn can affect the way they respond to the values and traditions of others.

When thinking about culture it is important to remember that no culture endorses child abuse. When working with 'children in need' from various cultural backgrounds it is important to remember that making false assumptions about cultures may put children at risk and that failing to acknowledge the family's strengths may also weaken the interventions that may be possible.

Using this book as an introductory guide will help practitioners and managers to better understand their safeguarding duties and responsibilities which, in turn, will ensure effective intervention if and when the need arises to take steps to protect a child.

Section One
What you need to know about child abuse

Chapter One **The legal and policy context**

Safeguarding children is everybody's business. We all share a common duty to ensure that children are protected from abuse and exploitation. If we have information or a suspicion that a child in our care, or who comes to our attention in other ways, is being ill-treated, it is not something we can just ignore. Doing nothing, or assuming that it is someone else's responsibility, is not an option. For practitioners working within early years, acting to stop or prevent abuse in its early stages, and helping a family to cope better may prevent a situation from escalating in a way that might have severe consequences for the child.

Early years practitioners are undoubtedly 'front line' staff in terms of safeguarding children; they are the ones who see children and their parents every day and are often the first to notice if things are not right. How efficiently they respond to their concerns is critical in ensuring the task of protecting the child is carried out effectively by the local authority's children's social care team.

In order for the work of safeguarding children to be carried out effectively there is a legal framework as well as guidance from the government to ensure every professional and every agency working with children of all ages understands their role and responsibilities. This also requires a sound knowledge base of child development as well as of the signs and signals or indicators of abuse and of what to do if they suspect abuse is taking place.

'Doing nothing, or assuming that it is someone else's responsibility, is not an option.'

The key pieces of legislation that frames and supports the safeguarding of children are summarised below.

The Children Act 1989

This Act came as a landmark in the protection of children as it set out new principles to guide the work of local authorities and the courts. The most important of which are:

- Paramount principle: The welfare of the child is paramount and must remain the focus of all intervention work and should not be sidelined through shifting the focus onto the needs of adults in the family.
- Parental responsibility: This marked a shift away from the idea of parental rights over their children towards their responsibility for them. The definition of parental responsibility and who has it is detailed in a later chapter of this book.
- Families are the best people to bring up children: Rather than the state intervening to remove children, families should first be helped to change and improve the way they care for their children. Resources should be allocated for this supporting and preventative work. Only if this fails should a child be removed.

This Act also provided a definition of 'significant harm' as the threshold for intervention into the private lives of families. It also established a definition for a child being 'in need' of services and the duties of the local authority in providing these. These definitions are set out in Chapter Four.

The key section of the Act which sets out the duty and power of the local authority to investigate concerns that a child may be being ill-treated is Section 47. S47 places a duty on local authorities to investigate where it has 'reasonable cause to suspect a child in their area is suffering, or is likely to suffer, significant harm'. S31(9) defines the term 'harm' as ill treatment or the impairment of health and development. The Adoption and Children Act 2002 amended this definition to include impairment suffered from seeing or hearing the ill treatment of another. Ill treatment includes sexual abuse and forms of ill treatment that are not physical.

Children Act 2004 - Every Child Matters

This legislation was introduced following Lord Laming's enquiry into the death of Victoria Climbié and provides the legal underpinning for the government's plan to transform services under the *Every Child Matters: Change for Children* programme. This has the ultimate aim of improving the co-ordination, delivery and effectiveness of services working to safeguard children. It also gives legislative weight to ensuring the five outcomes for all children are prioritised by all children's services across all sectors. These are to:

■ be healthy;

■ stay safe;

■ enjoy and achieve;

■ make a positive contribution; and

■ achieve economic well-being.

The main sections of this Act that have a bearing on the work of early years practitioners are Section 11 and 13 to 16. Section 11 of the Act places a duty on agencies with a responsibility towards children to carry out their functions with regard to the need to safeguard and promote the welfare of children. They must also make sure that any agency providing services on their behalf must do the same. Sections 13 to 16 make provision for the setting up of Local Safeguarding Children Boards (LSCB) comprising a statutory membership of local authority and health partners, police, courts and others relevant bodies to ensure co-ordinated services across local areas. The LSCBs have a remit for ensuring procedures are in place and that training is available for all practitioners in their area.

Safeguarding guidance for practitioners and agencies

The government sets out the main guidance for practitioners as follows.

What to do if you are worried a child is being abused (HMG 2006)

This sets out the procedures and process to be followed in all cases as the basis for national consistency in how child protection referrals are dealt with. There is also a summary publication as well as a flow chart for easy reference. This is an essential resource for every setting.

Statutory guidance on making arrangements to safeguard and promote the welfare of children under section 11 of the Children Act 2004 (HMG 2007)

This guidance is aimed at chief executives and senior managers in large organisations to ensure they have effective systems at a strategic level to support the task of safeguarding children. For example, for safe recruitment practices or systems for sharing information and accountability through the organisation and ensuring staff are trained to do the job. This is essential reading for senior officers in early years provider organisations.

Working Together to Safeguard Children- A guide to interagency working to safeguard and promote the welfare of children (HMG 2010)

Sets out the broader context for safeguarding including the roles and responsibilities for agencies and how they should work together. It provides definitions and thresholds for abuse as well as defining other factors that make children vulnerable in the wider society including crimes committed specifically against children. This most recent update came after Lord Laming's review and recommendations arising from that into the effectiveness of safeguarding measures. This is essential reading for those in early years settings or organisations who are designated child protection officers, lead professionals or senior operational managers.

Information Sharing: Guidance for practitioners and managers (HMG 2008)

It is important that practitioners share information in a way that is consistent with the Data Protection Act, and provide a sound basis for building knowledge about a child's situation in order to decide whether or not abuse is or may be taking place. It sets out definitions for what is confidential information, the situations when it may be shared, when consent should be sought and when consent may be overridden.

Chapter Two **Prevalence of child abuse - how widespread is it?**

The following key child protection statistics were compiled by the NSPCC in 2007, and are available on their website www.nspcc.org.uk.

Death of children through homicide in England and Wales

- On average, every week in England and Wales one to two children are killed at the hands of another person.

- Each week at least one child dies from cruelty.

- Infants under one year of age are more at risk of being killed at the hands of another person than any other age group of child under 18.

- Almost two-thirds of children killed at the hands of another person are under five years of age.

- Every ten days one child is killed at the hands of their parent.

- On average, 11 children per year are killed at the hands of strangers.

- Killings of children by a natural parent are committed in roughly equal proportions by mothers (47%) and fathers (53%), but where the child is killed by someone other than a parent, males strongly predominate.

- The proportion of child homicides in which the perpetrator is a parent is exceptionally high among infants.

- The proportion of child homicides where the parent is the principal suspect falls as children get older.

Child physical abuse, emotional abuse and neglect in the UK

- A quarter of children experience one or more forms of physical violence during childhood. For the majority of these children, the abuse happens at home and breaches 'acceptable societal standards'.

- In total, 21% of children experience some degree of physical abuse at the hands of their parents or carers during childhood.

- 7% of children experience serious physical abuse at the hands of parents or carers.

- The person responsible for physical violence during childhood was most often the mother (49%) or father (40%).

- 6% of children experience serious absence of care at home.

- 5% of children experience serious absence of parental supervision.

- 6% of children experience frequent and severe emotional maltreatment by their parents or carers.

- Nearly 32,000 children in the UK are known to be currently at risk of abuse.

- As at 31 March 2006, there were 31,919 children on the child protection registers in the UK.

- On average, over 700 registrations are made to child protection registers in the UK each week.

- With the exception of sexual abuse, both mothers and fathers are equally likely to be involved in the maltreatment of their children (physical abuse, emotional abuse and neglect).

- Studies into the prevalence of maltreatment among children with disabilities in the US have found that disabled children are over three times more likely to experience abuse and neglect than non-disabled children.

Child sexual abuse in the UK

- 1% of children aged under 16 experienced sexual abuse by a parent or carer, and a further 3% by another relative.

- 11% of children aged under 16 experienced sexual abuse by people known but unrelated to them.

- 5% of children aged under 16 experienced sexual abuse by an adult stranger or someone they had just met.

- In total, 16% of children aged under 16 experienced sexual abuse during childhood.

- Overall, 11% of boys and 21% of girls aged under 16 experienced sexual abuse during childhood.

- The majority of children who experienced sexual abuse had more than one sexually abusive experience.

- Three-quarters of sexually abused children did not tell anyone about the abuse at the time. 27% told someone later. Around a third still had not told anyone about their experiences by early adulthood.

- More than one third (36%) of all rapes recorded by the police in England and Wales are committed against children under 16 years of age.

- In 2002 in England and Wales, 45% of all rapes and attempted rapes that resulted in a criminal conviction were committed against children under 16.

- For the children who experienced sexual abuse in the family, the most common perpetrator was a brother or step-brother (38%), followed by a father (23%), by an uncle (14%), by a step-father (13%), by a cousin (8%), by a grandfather (6%) and by a mother (4%).

- For children who experienced sexual abuse outside of the family, the most common perpetrator was a boyfriend or girlfriend (70%), followed by 'someone I recently met' (17%), by a fellow student/pupil (10%), by a friend of their parents (6%) and by a friend of their brother or sister (6%).

- Very few children (less than 1%) experienced abuse by a professional in a position of trust.

'Every ten days one child is killed at the hands of their parent.'

We can conclude from these statistics that while many children do have normal happy lives, there is a significant minority for whom that is not the case. The figures for infant deaths by homicide suggest how critical early year services are as they are in a position to notice when things are not right and ensure children are safeguarded.

Protecting children from abuse is difficult work and is often upsetting and stressful. But it is also rewarding when parents who were in difficulty have got back on track and their children are no longer at risk. However, no child should remain in a highly abusive or dangerous situation and may need to be placed with and cared for by someone other than their birth parents, such as another family member or foster carer. Being paced with a foster carer is never a long term solution, agencies need to plan for that child to make a home situation safe for them to return to, or move them on to being adopted.

Looked after children

'Looked after' is the term used to describe when the local authority takes over the care of a child. There are two ways that a local authority may provide care for the child:

■ Voluntary: Accommodation may be provided by the local authority on a voluntary basis, for example, the parent has to go into hospital and there is no one else to look after the child. The parent can withdraw the child at any time.

■ Court Order: These may be an Emergency Protection Order, Police Protection, Remand, or an Interim or Full Care Order. A parent may not remove a child if he or she is subject to a legal order.

Very young children are no longer placed in children's homes, rather with another relative or with foster carers. Children's homes are more commonly used for older children, particularly those with challenging behavioural or psychological needs.

Chapter Three **Duties of early years settings**

Settings required to register under the Childcare Act 2008 must meet the Welfare Requirements of the Early Years Foundation Stage which sets out the statutory duties of the provider in relation to Safeguarding Children. The overarching requirement is:

The provider must take steps to safeguard and promote the welfare of children.

The specific legal requirements include:

- Implementing an effective safeguarding policy and procedure that is made known to parents.

- Informing Ofsted immediately if an allegation is made against a member of staff or anyone living or working on the premises, regardless of where the alleged abuse has taken place. The provider must give Ofsted an account of what allegedly happened and what they have done about it. It is an offence not to do this.

- Informing children's social care, the police or any other body in the provider's local area, identified by the Local Safeguarding Children's Board, of any allegations of abuse as above.

- Keeping allegations or concerns about abuse confidential- that means sharing the information only with the statutory agencies as above.

- Ensuring all staff understand the setting's procedures to follow if an allegation is made against a staff member, or anyone living or working on the premises.

- Appointing a 'designated person' to take the lead responsibility for safeguarding children within the setting. This person must attend training on child protection and must be able to liaise with statutory children's services agencies.

   Within this liaison duty the Alliance incorporates supporting staff in recognition of abuse, making timely and correct referrals, contributing to child protection meetings and to the child protection plan. This booklet will help the designated child protection person to do that.

Providers should also have regard to statutory guidance, including:

■ Ensuring practitioners have an up-to-date understanding of safeguarding children issues.

■ Ensuring staff are able to implement the setting's safeguarding children policy and procedures.

■ Ensuring the setting's policies and procedures are in line with the local LSCB guidance and procedures; these will be based on *What to do if you are worried a child is being abused (HMG 2006).*

■ Ensuring staff are able to respond appropriately to:

- significant changes in a child's behaviour;

- deterioration in their general well-being;

- unexplained bruising, marks or signs of possible abuse;

- neglect; and

- the comments made by children that give cause for concern.

This publication addresses these requirements. It will also provide useful background and procedures to guide practitioners in settings that are not required to be registered under the Childcare Act 2008, such as some crèches, drop-in groups or home visiting schemes.

'Staff are able to implement the setting's safeguarding children policy and procedures.'

Chapter Four Understanding Significant Harm

Definitions

Safeguarding work uses specific terminology that is defined legally; in this way it makes meanings clear so there cannot be confusion or misunderstanding of what different professionals mean.

- Child: Any child under the age of 19.

- Young person: Child aged 16-19 years, or 21 if child has a disability**.

- Child abuse: This is defined in s47 of the Children Act 1989 and refers to any situation where the child is, or is likely to, suffer 'significant harm'. It is further defined in *Working Together to Safeguard Children* (2010) and is discussed further below.

- Child in need: This is defined in s17 of the Children Act 1989. A child is defined as being a child in need if:

  - they are unlikely to achieve or maintain, or have the opportunity of achieving, or maintaining, a reasonable standard of health or development without the provision for them of services by a local authority; or

  - their health or development is likely to be significantly impaired or further impaired, without the provision of such services; or

  - they are disabled. (s17.10 Children Act 1989)

In deciding whether a child is 'in need' the local authority should consider the outcome for the child if no service is provided and the outcome on health and development if it was provided.

**The inclusion of children and young persons up to 19 years of age, or 21 if they have a disability, further extends the remit of settings beyond those of children under the age of five years. It is self evident that settings catering for children over the age of five will be using their procedures to cover all the age range catered for. However, even though settings may not be providing services where young people are the main recipients, they still have a duty of care towards young people as students or employees as well as young parents who may disclose abuse, either current or in the past. The procedures for this are the same as for reporting a concern involving any other child.

What is 'significant harm'?

Section 47 of the Children Act 1989 introduces the concept of 'significant harm' as the threshold that justifies the compulsory intervention into family life by the local authority in the best interests of children. There are no absolute criteria to define significant harm although there is clear agreement that the focus is on the impact of harmful behaviours on the child.

Sometimes significant harm may be the result of a single violent or traumatic act; more often it may be a culmination of a number of acts, including physical, emotional or sexual abuse, against the child that have an accumulating effect on the physical and psychological well-being of the child over time. It may also arise through the long term effects of neglect of their health or developmental needs.

The role of children's social care is to examine the evidence about the nature and degree of the abuse as well as to take account of the child's own perception of their safety against other risk and protective factors. A risk factor might include the parent's inability to protect their child or prevent harm, or inability to acknowledge and respond to the child's emotional or other needs. Protective factors might include the ability and willingness of the parents to recognise their child's needs and to take action to stop the abuse and develop more appropriate parenting. Other protective factors might include the support for a family through extended family or friendship networks or intervention of other services. It is the purpose of the *Assessment Framework* to identify all of the factors and weigh up the whole situation before deciding on a plan to promote the child's safety and best interests. This might begin with the Initial Assessment at referral stage or may start with an earlier Common Assessment or CAF being undertaken before the referral when concerns had not yet identified possible significant harm.

'Risk factors might include the parent's inability to protect their child or prevent harm.'

The contribution of those persons and agencies with direct contact with children and their families is invaluable in helping to make an assessment as accurate as possible. Therefore the role of the early years practitioner is crucial, as they are the people who see the child, and the family, daily and over long periods of time. They are in a good position to have considerable insight as to what is going on, as well as be in a good position to support the family on a day-to-day basis.

The Children Act 1989 (S31(9)) as amended by the Adoption and Children Act 2002 defines the following terms:

- Harm: means ill-treatment or the impairment of health or development, including impairment suffered from seeing or hearing the ill-treatment of another.

- Development: means physical, intellectual, emotional, social or behavioural development.

- Health: means physical or mental health.

- Ill-treatment: includes sexual abuse and forms of ill-treatment which are not physical.

Chapter Five **The four categories of child abuse**

In this section, each category of abuse is defined according to the definition in Working Together to Safeguard Children (HMG 2010). The 'signs' are the tangible things that you can see or detect and the 'signals' are those clues that may be expressed as behaviour or may be as a result of a direct or indirect disclosure.

The term 'indicator' is sometimes used instead of signs and signals but the term 'symptoms', which was once used, is less common now as child abuse is not a disease.

Physical abuse

This may take the form of hitting, punching, kicking, biting, burning, suffocating or scalding. It may involve the use of objects such as belts, sticks or other implements. Physical harm may also take the form of fabricating, or deliberately inducing, illness in a child. Physical abuse of children often co-exists with domestic abuse. Hitting children may arise as punishment in extreme displays of coercive discipline.

The signs of physical abuse are often the most easy to detect. Bruises, scald or burn marks, abrasions and fractures are the most common signs. Such signs are not always on visible parts of the body but unless you see them through the normal course of practice, such as nappy changing or supervising children getting changed for any other legitimate reason, practitioners should never undress a child to look for bruising. If you suspect a child has got injuries that are below their clothing, report your reasons for suspecting. Only a doctor can physically examine a child.

The signals invariably manifest as aggression, behavioural problems and poor achievement.

In the long term physical abuse can be linked to neurological damage, physical injuries that lead to disability. Almost always, emotional, behavioural and educational problems may persist unless skilled help is sought for the child.

Emotional abuse

Emotional abuse is defined as 'the persistent emotional maltreatment of a child such as to cause severe and persistent adverse effects on the child's emotional development'. It almost always accompanies any other kind of abuse, but can also occur alone. It involves the consistent undermining of the child's sense of self-worth and self-esteem, making the child feel unloved, worthless and inadequate, or only of value in as far as they meet the needs of another person. It may include silencing a child, not giving credibility to their views or ridiculing them. It may include developmentally inappropriate expectations being made on the child or having expectations that are too high, or by not allowing the child to explore and learn, being overprotective of them and restricting normal social interactions.

Emotional abuse may also involve witnessing or hearing the abuse of another. In this category also lies bullying, including cyber-bullying or the exploitation or corruption of children.

The signs of emotional abuse are less visible, but can be observed in the parent's treatment of the child, his or her responses to the child, how the child's feelings are acknowledged or otherwise and the parent's view and expectations for the child. In older children depression and self-harm may be evident.

The signals for emotional abuse are reflected in the child's sense of themselves as unworthy and unloved. They may show visible signs of fear and anxiety; they may lack confidence or social skills. The impact is especially severe in the early years. Behaviour may vary from extremes of being withdrawn and uncommunicative to being aggressive and angry. Emotional abuse may be a consequence of other problems within the family such as domestic violence, drug/alcohol abuse or parent's mental health problems where the parent is emotionally unavailable or unable to predict and meet their child's emotional needs.

In the long term, emotional abuse has a lasting damaging effect on psychological well-being and it must be noted that there is an element of emotional abuse in all other categories of abuse.

Sexual abuse

Sexual abuse involves 'forcing or enticing a child or young person to take part in sexual activities, whether or not the child is aware of what is happening'. It may or may not involve levels of violence. It may involve penetrative acts (vaginal, anal or oral penetration) and non-penetrative acts (masturbation, kissing inappropriately, rubbing or touching on the outside of clothing) as well as 'non-contact activities' such as engaging children in watching pornography or photographing them naked or in sexual acts with other children. It may involve grooming a child in preparation for abuse (including via the internet). Sexual abuse may be committed by females as well as males.

The signs of sexual abuse are more visible when penetrative acts have occurred and will show as genital or anal soreness or abrasions, infections and pain. There may be signs of urinary tract infections, or signs of sexually transmitted infections. However, not all cases involve such clear physical signs.

The signals that alert to the possibility of sexual abuse include sexualised behaviour, showing knowledge of sexual matters beyond a child's normal understanding for that age, or other aspects of disturbed emotional behaviour, such as sadness and shame, depression or aggression. Sometimes the behaviours may seem more bizarre such as soiling and smearing faeces or wetting themselves or having severe nightmares.

Sexual abuse is highly secretive and coercive. Children may be sworn to secrecy, on the threat of their lives or lives of others. This, coupled with the abuse, makes it all the more damaging to children's well-being. Once disclosed, the child's ability to cope is helped by having at least one non-abusing adult who believes the child who understands and can help to offer protection.

Neglect

Neglect is defined as the 'persistent failure to meet a child's basic physical and/or psychological needs, likely to result in the serious impairment of a child's health or development'. Neglect may occur during pregnancy as a result of maternal substance abuse. Neglect include parents or carers failing to provide adequate food, clothing and shelter, not protecting a child from harm or danger, or not responding to the child's health needs by failing to take the child for medical treatment or to ensure they attend school. It may also include failing to provide adequately for a child's emotional needs.

Signs of neglect include hunger, poor personal hygiene, inadequate clothing, being left indoors or outside alone or without supervision. Signs may also include extremes of impoverishment in the home, poor hygiene, lack of basic amenities such as heating, or bedding or no food.

The signals may show as impairment of normal growth and development, poor health, and, especially for older children, difficulties in forming relationships and low educational achievement or early encounters with the law.

'Long term difficulties with forming social relationships.'

Severe neglect has the effect of making it hard for children to form attachments, especially if the neglect starts from early infancy. It is also associated with serious impairment of intellectual development and physical growth. There may be long term difficulties with forming social relationships and educational progress. The extent of the effects of neglect depends on duration over time, the nature of the neglect and the age of the child at the time.

Chapter Six Parental factors affecting the vulnerability of children

The well-being of families may be affected by a number of social and circumstantial factors that affect their ability to cope and provide adequately for their children. It should be acknowledged that some of these factors are short term and more easily resolved with help and support, whilst others are longer term and more significantly damaging for children at the time, and as they become adults.

The stresses that parents face when bringing up children can have a negative effect on a child's health, development and well-being. The stresses that a mother may experience when pregnant as well as her ability to parent effectively, especially to respond to a baby's needs may also add to the vulnerability of her baby. This is exacerbated if there is no other supportive adult on hand to help.

Factors affecting vulnerability are taken into account when making an assessment of risk that a child may be, or is likely to, suffer significant harm. These factors include:

■ Social exclusion.

■ Domestic violence.

■ Mental illness.

■ Drug and alcohol abuse.

■ Parental learning disability.

Where one or more of these apply to families the likelihood or risk to children increases but it is not inevitable. There are protective factors which may mitigate against risk, such as:

■ Positive regard by parent of the child.

■ A strong family and supportive friendship network.

■ Access to community resources.

■ Improvement of the physical and material living conditions.

■ Opportunity, support and ability to address problems.

Social exclusion

Families that come to the attention of children's social care or other family welfare agencies to seek help and support often experience many social disadvantages. These may include severe poverty, social isolation, racism, or problems to do with living in a disadvantaged area. This could incorporate poor housing/homelessness, high crime, lack of childcare and access to basic amenities such as public transport, childcare, employment/training opportunities and lack of parks or leisure facilities. In some areas a lack of shops makes it hard to buy affordable, nutritious, fresh food. Poverty affects well-being of families at core levels of family life; poor diets lead to inadequate nutrition necessary for healthy growth and development and poor housing that is overcrowded or damp may affect children's health. Just the fact of having little money in itself creates stress that bears heavily on some parent's ability to cope. Substance abuse, depression, disability or long term mental or physical health problems all impact on the well-being of children in families experiencing social exclusion.

An additional factor for some of these families must be considered when children become carers for parents who are not able to care for themselves properly. According to the 2001 census there are some 175,000 young carers in the UK of which 5,000 are between the ages of five and seven years old. It can be assumed that in many cases the factors in their lives that define them as carers at the age of five are usually present much earlier in their lives.

What the early years setting should do

The role of the early years provision- whether a pre-school, day care or children's centre - can be most important in helping to break down isolation, provide support to parents and care and education for children that promotes their health and all round development. Where it is known or suspected that a child's parents may be experiencing one or many of the above factors that is affecting their capacity to parent effectively, the setting should make a referral to social care for support services for a 'child in need'. They should not assume that if a child is caring for a parent that other services will automatically have picked this up and should be aware of indicators such as older siblings collecting children on a regular basis because parents are unable to. They may use the Common Assessment Framework, where one is not already in place or where they have reason to believe that a child may be suffering, or is likely to suffer, significant harm as a result of the compounding effect of high level of social disadvantage, to make a referral to children's social care.

Domestic violence

Some 200,000 children live in households where there is a known risk of domestic violence. (Lord Laming 2009) It is known that when children witness or hear domestic violence over time, it can have a serious impact on their safety and welfare. Domestic violence is a feature in nearly half of the cases of child abuse that lead to a Serious Case Review.

Domestic violence often goes hand in hand with drug or alcohol abuse, mental health and a parental history of poor childhood experiences. Parental conflict that is fraught with tension may be as damaging as violence; violence is often accompanied by manipulative and controlling behaviour creating high levels of fear. The experience of violence may affect the ability to parent and is a contributor to mental health problems such as depression. Furthermore children are at physical risk themselves if they attempt to intervene or are used as a 'shield' to protect the victim of the violence. Onset of domestic violence commonly happens when a woman is pregnant or has a young baby. Domestic violence in pregnancy can put the foetus at risk of brain or other physical damage, and possibly miscarriage; violence may occur when the woman is nursing or holding the baby, putting the baby at direct risk of assault.

'200,000 children live in households where there is a known risk of domestic violence.'

The impact on children experiencing domestic violence can lead to anxiety or aggression, withdrawing or even running away. It cannot be underestimated at any age, and early years settings are in a position to be able to notice the signs of domestic violence and begin to approach a parent about it. Early years settings form close supportive networks with access to resources for help; the intimacy of relationships between staff and parents that grows over time often lead to a parent making a first disclosure to an early years member of staff.

Domestic violence may be suspected through the obvious signs of bruising or injuries, although great effort will be made to cover these up and attribute other causes. Frequency of injuries may be a sign that the injuries are not accidental, as well as absences while bruises fade or until the parent is able to venture out of the house.

Lord Laming (2009) *The Protection of Children in England: Progress Report*. London: The Stationery Office.

What the early years setting should do

The key message for early years practitioners is that domestic violence affects children deeply, even where no violence is directed against the child. Where this is suspected it must not be ignored and a referral to children's social care must be made in every case. Practitioners need to insist on the need for protection of the abused parent and even for themselves as reporters of the abuse. Practitioners should offer support to the non-abusing parent, and help to allay fears that reporting the abuse would mean their children being taken away. Social care is more concerned with supporting the non-abusing parent to take steps to protect the children and to get help for themselves.

If the parent who is experiencing the domestic violence refuses consent for the early years to share this information with social care, the setting must use their judgement in determining whether in not sharing the information will further put the parents and the child at risk of significant harm. Where this is felt to be the case, the setting may override the refusal to give consent, but they must inform the parent and record that they have made this decision and why. (Chapter Thirteen for details on information sharing.)

If the family are temporarily re-housed in a refuge the setting should keep in contact with children's social care with a view to keeping the early years place for the child to come back to when they return home or are re-housed. Children who witness domestic violence may require additional services to help them work through the emotional trauma; practitioners may note behaviour that causes concern and will need to work sensitively with the parent and the child to help them get over their experiences.

Mental illness

Nearly 30% of adults with mental illness have dependant children (Meltzer, D. 2003). A number of conditions can fall under the category of mental illness. These may include depression and anxiety or psychotic illnesses such as schizophrenia or bipolar disorder. It may also be associated with drug or alcohol abuse. Depression and anxiety are more commonplace with psychotic disorders less common. The effects on children may vary according to a number of factors and may not necessarily lead to adverse outcomes for a child. Support from a caring partner as well as good intervention from mental health services are factors that can help mitigate effects of the illness. However, all the factors need to be carefully assessed as the lack of support and management, as well as the severity of the condition, may lead to adverse effects on the child, including the need for the child to take on a caring role for the parent. Depression, especially post-natal depression, may cause a parent to be unable to respond to her baby as well as be able to provide safe physical care. This may lead to poor development in the early years and the unpredictability of the parent's responses may lead to children feeling bewildered or frightened. Psychotic conditions may result in hallucinations and difficulties with being able to tune in to the child's needs and feelings. In rare cases a child may be at risk of injury, neglect or death.

Meltzer, D. (2003) Inequalities in mental health: A systematic review. *The research findings register, Summary No. 1063*. London: Department of Health.

What the early years setting should do

Support to families is crucial especially where post natal depression is identified. An early years place may ease the pressure for the parent to enable them to seek treatment such as group therapy or counselling. It also provides a source of support for the parent, as well as their partner, in knowing they will receive a caring and non-judgemental response. Sometimes early years practitioners may be the first to notice that a parent seems depressed and unable to cope, or that they are saying or doing bizarre things. Making a referral to get help for the parent is crucial to ensure the well-being of the child and the family.

Parental problem use of drugs

Typically of most concern are parents who are users of crack cocaine and heroin; these may constitute less than 1% of the population. Due to the illegality of illicit drug use, it is hard to define exact numbers affected, but at least 1% of births each year are to women with problem drug use and 2 to 3% of children under 16 have parents with problem drug use. Almost twice as many mothers with problem drug use than fathers live with their children; children can also be affected by the drug use of a parent's new partner, a sibling or other person in the household. Experts on drug misuse warn against making assumptions on its impact on children for the following reasons:

- Different drugs vary in their effects.

- The same drug may have a different effect on different people.

- Personality factors influence the effects of the drug, such as existing mental illness or stressed state.

- Physiological factors may affect drug tolerance.

There are some parents whose drug misuse can be managed so as to reduce impact on families, and there are those who can also stop taking drugs and live well balanced lives. Many children with parents who misuse drugs do not have long term problems. Each case has to be viewed on its own standing and the parent's coping ability and effects of the misuse on the child or children must be considered.

When a parent's misuse of drugs leads to a chaotic lifestyle, where the priorities both financially and emotionally are turned towards the obtaining and taking of the drug, it can be expected that children may experience degrees of neglect and emotional abuse. Families may move house suddenly or frequently to get away from debt or may be subject to crime against them at worst or, at least, stigmatising by neighbours. A parent's mental capacity may be affected by the drug and when under the influence may be unresponsive, lack awareness of what is going on around them or lose consciousness altogether. A child may lack food and clothing, may be inadequately supervised or exposed to danger.

Drug use may affect an unborn child, so good ante-natal care is important although some pregnant women who misuse drugs may fear having to tell doctors about their problem and don't get the help for themselves and their unborn child that they need. Risks include low birth weight, premature birth or death in early infancy. For mothers who misuse drugs there is an impact on attachment and the ability to respond empathically to a baby or young child. Unpredictable mood swings may lead to anxiety as the baby or young child tries to work out what sort of a mood mum is in today and adjust accordingly.

Parental problem use of alcohol

Alcohol consumption is legal but misuse of alcohol through either binge drinking, habitual drinking or alcoholism, can have severe consequences. A survey of callers to Child Line (1997) report 57% identify father or a father figure as having a drink problem, approximately 30% identify the mother and 7% identify both parents.

The impact of excessive drinking on the capacity to parent, like drug misuse, depends on what is drunk and how much over what period as well as individual factors such as mental state or tolerance and reaction to alcohol. Excessive alcohol can inhibit behaviour that may lead to unpredictable reactions or violence; severe intoxication can cause sleepiness or coma or extremes of vomiting.

The highest risk associated with problem drinking is violence, particularly by the father or father figure, especially if violence begins towards the woman during the pregnancy.

Similar to mothers who misuse drugs, women with drink problems tend to avoid ante-natal care services. Heavy drinking in the early stages can cause miscarriage or in the later stages, Foetal Alcohol Syndrome, which may include growth deficiency for height and weight, distinct facial features and possible central nervous system disorders. There is a view now that Foetal Alcohol Syndrome (FAS) presents more as a Spectrum Disorder rather than as a distinct classification. The breadth of the spectrum would depend on maternal levels of drinking during pregnancy and it is now thought that relatively low levels of alcohol consumption can result in FAS symptoms. FAS is thought to affect about 4% of babies born to women who drink heavily.

Risks associated for babies born to mothers who misuse alcohol are lack of attention to baby's needs due to pre-occupation with own feelings or lack of capacity to engage with and stimulate the baby, keep the baby safe from harm or attend to his or her health needs. Insecure attachment and cognitive delay may arise from lack of attention and emotional warmth.

ChildLine (1997) *Beyond the limit: children who live with parental alcohol misuse*. London: ChildLine.

What the early years setting should do

Support services are vital to break isolation and provide a safe anchor for a parent who misuses drugs or alcohol. Provision of a child care place will help provide a child with a safe environment, nutrition, a caring and attentive key person as well as opportunities for play. It is important to recognise the difficulty that some parents who misuse drugs or alcohol will have in just getting into the early years setting on time, especially for settling the child in. Support for the parent from a drug agency or family support service, perhaps to offer practical help, for example, in household tasks or getting children to the nursery, is critical in ensuring the placement is able to fully benefit the child.

Early years staff need to be sensitive to the feelings of inadequacy or guilt that mothers who misuse drugs or alcohol have about their situation, so non-judgemental attitudes that are accepting of the person and that ensure no parent is ostracised because of their problems will help to build trust and self-esteem. Outcomes are better if there is one parent who is not misusing drugs or alcohol and where the parent who does misuse recognises they have a problem and is willing to receive help.

Giving up drug or alcohol misuse is hard and, if there are sufficient stressful factors, these may trigger possible relapses even after long periods of abstinence. No matter how hard a parent may appear to be trying to manage or overcome their drug or alcohol misuse and no matter how committed early years staff are to offering help and support to the parent, if the child appears to be suffering neglect or seems to be in an endangered situation or otherwise at risk of significant harm, a referral to children's social care must be made or a report made to the social care worker where there is one already allocated. The setting's role and responsibilities in this case must be made clear to parents from the start; it is the child's well-being that is paramount and must be protected even where that may have implications that are uncomfortable for the parent.

Settings should bring any concerns they may have about a child's possible emotional or developmental problems to the attention of support agencies for the family; good observation based child development records are essential in highlighting any potential problems that may require additional support.

Parents with learning disabilities

There are many different causes for, and a wide spectrum of, learning disabilities in adults. The effects may vary but in each case the disability is life long. The Department of Health (Cm 5086 2001) defines learning disability as including:

- A significantly reduced ability to understand new or complex information or learn new skills (impaired intelligence); with

- A reduced ability to cope independently (impaired social functioning).

- An onset before adulthood and having lasting effect on development.

Cm 5086 (2001) *Valuing People: A New Strategy for Learning Disability for the 21st Century*. London: The Stationery Office. Cm 5086 2001, p.14, paragraph 1.5.

29

There are just under a million people in the UK with a learning disability, roughly equating to 2% of the population. Of these up to 25% may be parents, many of which manage being parents well enough with good support so it is important not to make assumptions that having a learning disability pre-disposes towards child abuse in any way. Although a lack of support may result in some degree of neglect and this risk may increase where there are other stress factors involved, such as having a disabled child, poor health, domestic violence or a history of growing up in care etc.

Parents with a learning disability may be inadequately prepared for the birth; some may not recognise the signs of pregnancy. They may not receive ante-natal care until later in the pregnancy and may not be able to understand or act on the health advice given. Mothers may not understand a baby's feeding needs or find it hard to establish a routine, recognise illness or provide good supervision of mobile babies. Some may find it hard to engage or stimulate their baby's learning and some may leave the baby with an unsuitable person, not realising the dangers.

Support from the wider family can make a positive difference to outcomes, as well as support services such as an early years place. Specialist assessment needs to be carried out in order for social care and other agencies to make informed decisions about the level and type of support that would benefit. Multi-agency and multi-disciplinary assessments give the broadest picture; group education and home based support based on assessment gives the best results.

What the early years setting should do

The early years setting would be part of a multi-agency team and have their part to play. In larger children's centres there may be an opportunity to provide group work or education facilities for parents with learning disabilities, but for nurseries and pre-schools, ensuring parents with learning disabilities have access to all services, attend events and take as full a part in day-to-day early years life is essential in promoting an inclusive approach. The setting, especially the child's key person, should be fully involved in a multi-agency team, contributing information about the child's development and their view of the parent's capacity as well as carrying out key tasks as determined by the team. A concern may arise where a practitioner suspects the child's needs are not being met or where there appears to be a gap in the services provided, leaving the child vulnerable and at risk of significant harm. It may also be the case that the child or older siblings are taking on an increased role in caring for the parent and appear not to have sufficient support around them. The procedure for reporting concerns, as agreed by the multi-agency team, should be followed.

Chapter Seven Other ways children may suffer significant harm

Working Together to Safeguard Children (HMG 2010) summarises additional supplementary guidance on other distinct ways that children encounter abuse or exploitation that will lead to them suffering significant harm. These are described below in the order of likelihood that they might occur in the early years or the likelihood of the child attending an early years setting where they may be suspected. Where these are suspected, referral to children's social care should always be made.

Kinds of abuse that may come to light in an early years setting

Kinds of abuse that may come to light in an early years setting may include:

- Abuse of disabled children.

- Fabricated or induced illness.

- Child abuse linked to belief in spirit possession.

- Sexually exploited children.

- Female genital mutilation.

Indicators of abuse of disabled children

Evidence in the UK shows that disabled children are at increased risk of abuse and neglect. This may be because disabled children may be more likely to:

- be socially isolated;

- be more dependant on parents and carers for supporting daily living, including intimate personal care, which may increase risk of exposure to abuse;

- have impaired capacity- physically or mentally - to resist or avoid abuse;

- have speech, language or communication difficulties which make it hard for them to tell someone what is happening;

- not have access to someone they can trust and to disclose abuse to; and

- be vulnerable to bullying or intimidation.

What the early years setting should do

Practitioners in early years settings should work as part of a multi-agency team, alongside parents of a disabled child. They are well placed to have daily contact with parents and identify concerns as they arise. A parent may show ambivalence towards the child, or play down the effect of the disability; they may not turn up for appointments or show signs of not coping with the stressful demand of a disabled child, especially if there are other children in the family or the disabled child's behaviour or complex level of need is challenging. Parents may be stressed through also trying to meet the needs of their disabled child to the best of their ability and not recognise their own needs for time away or support. For families, where there is a disabled child, they may have less income if one parent cannot work, are more likely to experience social exclusion and family breakdown is common. Even parents who cope well and love their child, accepting his or her disability, may still be prone to self blame and times of anguish.

The early years setting is well placed to offer support in a friendly and non-judgemental way, giving time and space for the parent to talk about their day-to-day concerns, as well as provide an emotionally nurturing, safe and stimulating environment for the child. They may contribute enormously to improving developmental and behavioural outcomes for the child.

The practitioners who are close to the family, such as the child's key person or support worker, might notice signs or signals of abuse in much the same way as for any other child and will follow procedures for referral or for reporting as for any other child protection concern.

'Well placed to offer support in a friendly and non-judgemental way.'

Indicators of fabricated or induced illness (FII)

A parent who deliberately makes up or causes illness in their child often appears as extremely caring and genuinely worried for their child. What characterises FII is a lack of the usual corroboration of findings with symptoms or signs, i.e. tests show up as negative, the reported symptoms don't fit the picture for known conditions or the symptoms don't get better after usual treatments. Sometimes the parent may report new symptoms after previous ones have been resolved and very often symptoms are not seen by other carers. The parent may go to extremes to protect the child from further illness, such as keeping them home from the childcare setting or not allowing them to do certain activities, thus limiting their normal lives. A parent may fabricate a medical history, or falsify specimens or test results or deliberately cause symptoms in various ways.

FII is extremely complex behaviour that has a number of causes, including severe stress, and should not to be confused with a parent who seems overanxious about his or her child's health or who feels his or her child has been misdiagnosed or that the child's symptoms are not being taken seriously. This is common for many parents. A diagnosis of FII can only take place over time as the medical picture evolves and discrepancies are picked up by medical staff and trained experts in this condition.

What the early years setting should do

Severe stress within a family, particularly domestic violence, is known to be linked with FII, so where a referral has been made, often by medical staff, to children's social care, offering support services as part of a s47 assessment may include provision of a child care place. The manager and key person would be briefed and the parent would be clear as to what the setting knows and what their role is in relation to reporting any further concern. The role of the early years setting would be to keep close observation of the child's general health and possibly keep a daily record; it would also be helpful to support the parent in helping to gain confidence in their child's good health.

If the concerns regarding a parent's management of their child's health needs arise from the setting suspecting that the child's illness is fabricated or induced they should report their concerns, backed up by evidence from their case records, in the usual way. This concern may arise when the parent's description of the child's health problems does not ring true with the practitioner's day-to-day observations of the child. The parent may be bringing in a number of medicines which raises concern with the staff who may doubt their legitimate origin as being prescribed for the child. The child may be being taken for a large number of hospital appointments or missing early years sessions because of the parent's concerns. When referring to children's social care, as in any other circumstance, the practitioner would discuss concerns with the parent unless they felt it would put the child at further risk of significant harm. They should not try to contact the child's GP or health visitor to discuss their concerns, which should only go via children's social care.

Indicators of child abuse linked to belief in 'spirit possession'

Beliefs in 'possession' or fears of 'witchcraft' are widespread across many countries and cultures. The number of identified cases is small, but the nature of this kind of abuse means it may have severe consequences for physical, emotional and psychological health.

A child may become the 'scapegoat' in a family, blamed for misfortunes, or have a developmental or behavioural difficulty that is not understood and is attributed to 'witchcraft' or 'possession' by an 'evil force'. Attempts are made to 'exorcise' or 'deliver' the child, often through violent or psychological means that may also be bizarre, involving isolation and humiliation of the child. It may occur where the family is under duress or where the child is living with carers who are not his or her birth parents; it is often linked to mental ill-health of the perpetrator. In some cases it may be a faith leader or other 'spiritual healer' who is charged with carrying out the abusive 'exorcism' on behalf of the family.

What the early years setting should do

It is good practice in any setting that some basic information about each child's cultural and religious background is taken when the child starts the setting. As a matter of course, practitioners will also record details of who has parental responsibility, or who other main carers might be, as part of the registration process. They may at this time find out if the child is privately fostered or has been living away from home for any period of time. This information may provide a valuable background context for identifying beliefs in 'spirit possession'.

The practitioners in an early year setting may begin to suspect child abuse through seeing signs of physical abuse or neglect, signs of emotional disturbance, neglect and poor attendance. The child may disclose that they have been told they are 'evil' or similar and may describe what has happened to them to rid them of the 'possession'. They may be afraid and disoriented. They may disappear suddenly, i.e. be taken out of the early years setting suddenly without a word, and the parents may not respond to attempts to make contact. If abuse of this nature is suspected, a referral should be made in the usual way, after discussion with the parents, as long as you are sure this will not put the child at further risk of harm.

Indicators of sexually exploited children

Any child who is the victim of sexual exploitation is suffering sexual abuse. In the case of young children, they may have been abused through the misuse of technology; where photographs and or videos have been taken of them that are of a sexual nature, either for personal satisfaction or for distribution personally or electronically, with or without money changing hands. They may be abused through criminal gang activity or through trafficking, but these children are less likely to be attending a registered child care facility (whether group care or childminder) unless the facility itself has been infiltrated by abusers for the purpose of sexually exploiting children.

What the early years setting should do

If an early years practitioner suspects the behaviour of a colleague or colleagues might indicate sexual exploitation of children, he or she must refer their concerns to children's social care using a 'whistle blowing' process. It is not recommended to discuss this with colleagues or the manager as the practitioner may not know who else is involved. The reporting practitioner should record evidence that backs their concerns, but should not wait to try to get more evidence where it appears scanty as children may continue to be abused during that time.

Each setting should have procedures in place that do not allow staff to take mobile camera phones into group rooms, and which state precisely the purpose for which children may be filmed or photographed, such as for the child's developmental records, or other legitimate purpose for which parents have given consent. Cameras and memory cards used within the setting should be only those bought for use in the stated way, and images then stored on the setting's computer where the password is known only to staff.

Indicators of female genital mutilation

Female genital mutilation (FGM) is a criminal offence, making it an offence for UK nationals or permanent residents to carry out FGM in this country or take a child out of the country in order to carry out the procedure. It is also an offence to aid or abet or procure the procedure abroad even in countries where it is otherwise legal. It is practised in 28 African countries, parts of the Middle and Far East, but is also carried out in Western countries where there are communities coming from countries where it is practised. It is estimated that 24,000 girls under the age of 15 are at risk of FGM in the UK. Parents do not carry this out with intent to abuse as they may believe it is the girl's best interest in their culture.

Female genital mutilation (FGM) refers to a procedure that may include the removal of part or all of the external female genitalia for cultural or other non-therapeutic reasons. The procedure is painful, medically unnecessary and will have serious health consequences for the child at the time as well as into the future, especially in childbirth. It may be carried out in girls as young as four years and up to thirteen years, but it can also take place at birth or before marriage. A number of girls die through blood loss or infection caused by the procedure.

What the early years setting should do

Whilst it is less common for a very young girl to be put through this procedure, it is not to be ruled out. A setting might suspect a young child from a community practising FGM is at risk of FGM by the child disclosing they are going abroad for a special reason or the child may return from their family's country of origin with noticeable behaviour changes or complaining of health problems, for example when urinating. They may notice abnormalities of external genitalia when changing a younger child if the procedure was carried out at birth. The setting might hear that a trip is being planned for an older sister where FGM is suspected as the reason for that trip.

Where staff suspect that a girl may be being prepared for this procedure, or that it may have already been carried out, they should report their concerns to children's social care. They should not discuss this with the parent first as this may mean the child being taken out of the country sooner.

If a setting is in an area where there are communities who carry out this practice, they should work with their Local Safeguarding Children Boards to provide culturally sensitive information to families to help reduce its prevalence. The community education role is essential in curbing this practice and the early years setting or children's centre can have a part to play in that.

Other kinds of abuse which are less likely to be identified in an early years setting

The following kinds of abuse may be less likely to come to light in an early years setting but may nevertheless be suspected through another way, for example through local grapevines, older siblings or neighbour concerns. These include:

■   Children affected by gang activity.

■   Complex, multiple or organised abuse.

■   Forced marriage or honour based violence.

■   Child victims of trafficking.

Early years settings, especially those that are part of children's centres, are often at the hub of the community. Staff hear about things through what parents or children tell them or through their own experiences and concerns about living in the area themselves. The types of abuse listed below are less likely to be experienced by a child who lives with their family, who are part of the community and who have full time places in a setting. They may be experienced by children and young people who are marginalised and powerless or who have no-one to stand up for them.

Safeguarding, as described earlier in this book, is not just about the protection of individual children that come within our sphere of professional activity, but it is about our wider awareness of injustices that affect children and knowing what to do if we come across that in any aspect of our lives. Safeguarding children is about coming together as a community and as a society to ensure children are safe from harm. Each of the kinds of abuse below are linked to covert criminal activity and if anyone suspects that a child or children are affected by these things they should be able to know what to do.

Children affected by gang activity

Children who may be at risk of being drawn into gangs are likely to be older than those in an early years setting, but could be being groomed into gangs by older siblings or other children from as young as seven years. The risks here concern gang related violence, drugs, knife or gun crime and sexual violence.

A child may be affected as a victim or a perpetrator or both.

Children naturally seek out their peers to form friendships and 'hang out' with; what distinguishes healthy peer grouping from being involved in gangs is the link to criminal activity where displays of violence are characteristic of gang membership. Children who have had disrupted childhoods, who may well be the victims of long standing abuse and neglect, fail to develop empathy towards others and seek recognition and power through violent behaviours.

The early years setting is a secure base in a community where abuse or family difficulties can be recognised, and responded to so that essential support can be gained. Very young children who have troubled lives, who have already developed emotional and behavioural difficulties, should not be allowed to drift as their problems will not get better on their own. The early years setting has an important role to play in building a stable community where individuals feel a sense of belonging, where children are secure and valued and where parents form friendships and build strong community networks. All of these factors mitigate against children developing extremes of anti-social and violent behaviour later on.

Complex, multiple or organised abuse

This is defined as involving one or more abuser and a number of children. Abusers may be acting together, or in isolation or they may be using the framework of a kinship network or family, an organisation or setting, to draw in other abusers or recruit children for abuse. It can occur in residential establishments, such as children's homes or boarding schools as well as day care or youth clubs. Abuse through misuse of technology may also be linked to highly organised networks of abusers.

An early years setting may become suspicious if an unusual number of children seem to present with signs and signals of abuse; especially sexual abuse. They should make their observations and concerns known to children's social care if they feel there may be linking factors. The setting itself could also become vulnerable to infiltration by abusers who may act individually or with others to perpetrate abuse against children. A practitioner should never feel afraid to 'whistle blow' and report concerns to children's social care if they have reason to suspect organised abuse in this way.

Forced marriage or honour based violence

Honour based violence can happen in a number of communities and is usually linked to the idea that a family member has brought 'shame' or 'dishonour' on the family. Honour based violence is a human rights abuse and is covered by the government's definition of domestic violence. If you are concerned that a parent or other adult or young person may be at risk of such violence, do not try to discuss this with family members but contact the police and ensure that the potential victim is offered protection. It is unlikely that threats will have been made in vain, or that the perpetrator might calm down and change their mind.

Forced marriage is not the same as arranged marriage, where both parties agree or reject potential suitors that parents suggest. Forced marriage is coercive and there is no choice or opportunity to refuse. It may affect victims from many communities. Several hundred girls or young women are forced into marriages every year in the UK. It is not a crime in itself, but crimes may be committed in the process. Victims may be forcibly taken or abducted, threatened or assaulted. Sexual assault, whether the victim is married to the perpetrator or not, is a crime. Children as young as nine, but more commonly young women in their teen years may be forced into marriage either in the UK or abroad. They may be removed from school and kept imprisoned at home, or may believe that they are being taken on holiday and may, or may not, suspect the reason why.

If anyone confides in you that they fear a marriage is being arranged for themselves, or someone they know, they are likely to be extremely frightened both of the impending forced marriage and the repercussions of disclosing. Do not discuss the concern with any family member or friend of the family; mediation is rarely successful and often leads to honour based violence, even death. Record as much information as you can and report to children's social care or to the police. The individual concerned can apply for a Forced Marriage Protection Order as can those around her who wish to protect her.

Child victims of trafficking

The UK is a transit and destination country of trafficked children from many parts of the world. It involves a great deal of suffering for those children who are exploited through force, coercion, threats and deception. Reasons for trafficking children vary from domestic labour to sexual exploitation or involvement in criminal activity. It should not be confused with children who are sent by their parents to the UK to live with another member of the family, or bone fide private foster carers, for the genuine purpose of education or a better life.

Very young children may be trafficked for reasons of benefit fraud or immigration scams. Children may be received by those acting as 'foster carers'; such individuals are highly unlikely to be bone fide private foster carers who must register with the local authority and have a CRB check carried out.

It is unlikely that anyone involved in this kind of criminal activity would bring a trafficked child to an early years setting, but a practitioner may be alerted to a family's possible use of a child domestic servant. They may become suspicious about a household in their neighbourhood where children seem to come and go, always in secrecy. Any suspicions should be reported to children's social care or the police.

Chapter Eight **Roles and responsibilities of agencies**

There are many different agencies who have a part to play in safeguarding children. Their roles and responsibilities are set out in the government's guidance *Working Together to Safeguard Children* (HMG 2010). Their roles, responsibilities and contributions made to the safeguarding process are co-ordinated by the Local Safeguarding Children Board (LSCB) in each local authority. In this chapter the role of the LSCB is described as well as the role of certain key agencies that are most frequently involved in child protection casework that early years practitioners are likely to come across.

The Local Safeguarding Children Board (LSCB)

Local authorities are required by the Children Act 2004 to establish LSCBs in order to effectively co-ordinate safeguarding and promoting children's welfare in their area in a way that contributes to improving the five outcomes in Every Child Matters. The LSCB's key objectives include:

- Co-ordination of each person or body represented on the Board regarding safeguarding and promoting children's welfare in that area.

- Ensuring each person's contribution to that process is effective in meeting that aim.

- Carrying out preventative work where possible to avoid children suffering from harm.

There are three main strands to their remit.

1 Involvement in activity to identify and prevent maltreatment, or impairment of health or development and ensure safety of children. This includes promoting the message across communities that safeguarding is everybody's business including providing public information on where children and parents can go for help.

2 Involvement in pro-active work to develop thresholds and procedures for work with children and families where a child has been identified as 'in need' under the Children Act 1989 but not suffering or likely to suffer significant harm. This would include mechanisms to ensure Child Assessment Framework processes are carried out. It also includes focusing on children who are more vulnerable, such as those not living at home, runaways, or those in the youth justice system or who are affected by gang activity.

3 Responding to children who are suffering or likely to suffer significant harm, including:
   - Children abused in their families including those harmed in the context of domestic abuse or those harmed as a consequence of substance misuse or parental mental ill health.
   - Children abused outside of the family by adults known to them, by professional carers, by strangers, or other young people.
   - Children abused through sexual exploitation or who are young victims of crime.

LSCBs also have a role to play in ensuring there are plans in place to ensure children who have been identified as needing protection achieve planned developmental outcomes and to check that these plans are effective.

Training is a key responsibility of LSCBs, both for single agencies as well as multi-agency. They may provide training or ensure it is available; they must however evaluate training and ensure staff who need training are receiving it.

LSCBs also ensure there are robust procedures for the safe recruitment of those employed to work with children, including compliance with CRB checks and registration with the Independent Safeguarding Authority (ISA). Critically, they are also there to ensure that organisations have effective procedures for responding where allegations have been made against staff who work with children. They are also required to have procedures in place for co-operating with other local authorities and other Board partners.

Finally they have a critical role to play in relation to child deaths and to where there has been concern about how agencies have worked to protect a child.

'Ensure robust procedures for the safe recruitment of those employed to work with children.'

Membership of the Local Safeguarding Children Board is at a strategic senior level; it would include a statutory membership of elected members (i.e. councillors) and other local authority departments, such as Education, Social Care or Housing, the Police, Primary Care Trusts or other NHS Trusts, Youth Offending Team, Connexions, the Children and Family Courts Advisory service (CAFCAS), Governors of prisons or Secure Training Centres. Representation from relevant adult care services as well as lay members.

Roles and responsibilities of key agencies and professionals who work within them

Local authorities

Children's Social Care: Staff who work in children's social care have a key role to play in investigating where a child is suffering or is likely to suffer significant harm. They will undertake an assessment of the child's needs and the parent's capacity to meet those needs and keep the child safe.

Adult services: Have a part to play where they become aware of risks to a child, as a result of their work with an adult client, and a duty to share information with children's social care.

Housing authorities and registered social landlords: May come to hear of families, that are either in housing they provide or where families or children are homeless, who require welfare support.

Sport, culture and leisure services: Staff may be concerned about the possible activity of abusers through their services, such as parks or sports centres, and have a role to play in ensuring children are safe and that action is taken where there are concerns.

Connexions: They work with young people to provide advice, guidance and training and may develop concerns about a young person they work with. They are required to work closely with other agencies that support young people to protect and promote their well-being.

Health Services

General practitioner (GP) and dental services: Are required to register with the Care Quality Commission that will include standards for safeguarding and promoting the welfare of children. GPs are often the first point of contact for families with the health service and hold a thorough picture of the family's health needs and concerns. The Child Health Programme for 0-5 and 5-19 year olds identifies where there are health needs and ensures these, including complex needs, are met. This provides a mechanism for alerting GPs and health staff where a health need, or neglect of a health need, may lead to concerns about a child suffering or likely to suffer significant harm that must be reported to children's social care. Health visitors and school nurses have an important part to play in securing children's health through their considerable and valuable contact with children and their parents. Dentists may be alerted to abuse through routine dental examination.

Maternity services: While these ensure mothers have access to good ante-natal care to ensure the health of the mother during pregnancy as a key factor in promoting healthy babies, they are also aware of where there may be circumstances that mitigate against both and where the health and well-being of the unborn baby may be compromised, for example, where there may be domestic violence, drug or alcohol misuse, learning difficulties or mental health issues. It is estimated that a third of domestic violence starts, or escalates, in pregnancy. Maternity services can provide support and information for pregnant women where they feel safe to disclose and can act to protect themselves and their unborn child. They can also alert children's social care where they may have concerns that the baby may suffer significant harm arising from factors within the mother.

Child and adolescent mental health services (CAMHS): These services are designed to help children, young people and their families where there are mental health problems as a result of abuse or neglect. Children and young people may be referred from various agencies for various reasons, but where professionals feel there are child protection concerns they must alert children's social care. They are also a major contributor in the initial and subsequent assessment of children.

Adult mental health services: Where a patient with a mental illness is also a parent, there is a need to safeguard and promote the welfare of that child through working closely and sharing information with children's social care.

Alcohol and drug services: These services need to recognise the needs of clients who are also parents as well as the implications of their misuse of drugs or alcohol for children. Close working with health and social care helps promote the well-being of all family members and especially ensures that children's needs are not overlooked while focussing on the adult's problems.

Paediatricians: Mostly always involved with every child from birth and have a key role to play in early detection as part of routine screening, as well as honing in on the identification, diagnosis and intervention where concerns about physical and cognitive development arise and especially where child abuse is suspected as the cause.

Police and other services

Police and Child Abuse Investigation Units (CAIU): All police forces have a CAIU to take responsibility for investigating child abuse cases. However, all police are required to have awareness of a broader safeguarding remit and to know how to respond to suspected child abuse, especially where it may come to light as part of the investigation of another crime such as domestic violence. Gathering information about a family's relevant criminal record is an essential aspect of an s47 investigation, and children's social care make routine requests to their CAIU for this. CAIU officers are almost always involved in initial case conferences to establish whether concerns meet the threshold for a criminal investigation.

Probation services: Working with offenders that have not been given custodial sentences or those released from prison, their role is to support the offender to make sure they do not re-offend. Where the offender is also a parent they have an important part to play in the rehabilitation of the offender to make sure children in the family are not at risk from, or being drawn into, criminal activity.

Prisons: Prison staff have a role to play in helping prisoners to maintain family ties, as these are important both for prisoner rehabilitation and for ensuring the well-being of their family and particularly children. Family visiting is encouraged as well as play provision for children visiting a parent in prison. Some women's prisons have mother and baby units to promote attachment and bonding as well as good parenting to promote well-being of babies and their mothers in the longer term. All prison staff must be aware of those prisoners who pose a risk to children and follow procedures to ensure they do not have contact with children.

Secure estate/Youth offending: This incorporates secure residential accommodation for young offenders; staff working in such institutions have a duty to ensure children are protected against harm from themselves, staff or peers. Youth offending teams are non-custodial but have a role to play to identify children at risk of offending, recognising the child abuse may be a causal factor in offending behaviour.

UK Border Agency: This agency deals with immigration matters, including for children who have no right of entry or to remain in the UK. They have a particular detection and prevention role with regard to child trafficking or the detection of pornographic material involving children being smuggled into the country. They have a duty to ensure any child they come across who is suffering or likely to suffer significant harm receives appropriate social care services from their local authority.

Education

Schools and further education institutions: Schools provide almost universal services for all children and are a key agency in identifying concerns about child abuse and for reporting it to children's social care. They must have appropriate procedures and knowledge of child abuse and how to act on concerns. Further education institutions have a duty to protect any child up to the age of 18 and 21 for a disabled child. Schools and FE settings also have an educative role to play in helping children's personal development, self-esteem and healthy relationships as well as providing information and sources of help regarding abuse.

Early years services: These include childminders, pre-schools, day nurseries, children's centres, crèches and drop in provision and they must all meet the EYFS welfare requirements for safeguarding children in their care. It is essential that staff have knowledge of child abuse and what to do if they suspect it.

Other services

Children and family court advisory and support services (CAFCASS): This agency has a wide ranging role in relation to promoting interests of children though the courts, which could be in relation to adoption or deciding where the child should live after parental break up (residency). They may also be appointed by the court to act as a Children's Guardian in any case where there are legal proceedings involving a child.

The armed services: The Ministry of Defence has its own welfare arrangements concerning under 18's in the armed forces (including looked after under 18s) as well as families serving in the armed forces. There are arrangements in place for sharing information with children's social care who retain the ultimate responsibility for safeguarding and promoting the welfare of every child. Links are maintained with British Forces Social Work Services (Overseas) to maintain protection of children who are subject of a child protection plan. Similar links are in place with UK services and United States Forces stationed in the UK.

The voluntary sector: There are a large number of children's charities in the UK, some of whom work directly to provide services for children 'in need'. The only charity who may initiate proceedings to protect children other than the local authority is the NSPCC. Voluntary organisations work within communities and have a role to play in providing information to the public as well as practitioners about child abuse, its detection and prevention.

Faith based organisations: These come from all religious faiths and work with children and families in many kinds of ways in their communities. All must have knowledge of safeguarding matters and be able to address these matters by responding appropriately where concerns have been raised.

Any organisation, whether a statutory authority or a voluntary organisation must take steps to prevent abusers for seeking employment in their organisations, whether paid or voluntary, and in any capacity. All must adhere to safe recruitment practices, carry out CRB checks and ensure staff are registered with the Independent Safeguarding Authority(ISA). All organisations must have procedures for managing allegations against a staff member and for liaising with children's social care and the police. All are required to register any incident where a member of staff has been dismissed for actual or suspected harm to a child with the ISA.

Chapter Nine **Parental responsibility**

Definition

Parental responsibility is a concept that replaced the idea of 'parent's rights'. It was introduced by the Children Act 1989 and is defined in Part 1 Section 3 (1) as: 'all the rights, duties, powers and responsibilities and authority which by law a parent of a child has in relation to the child and his property.'

This is also extended to anyone who is a guardian of a child in certain circumstances.

Parental responsibility cannot be surrendered or transferred to someone else. It can only be ended on application to the Court by the person with parental responsibility or, with the Court's consent, by the child. Many people refer to 'Parental Responsibility' simply as 'PR'.

Who has parental responsibility?

- The biological mother of the child.

- Married fathers (who do not lose it even on divorce).

- Unmarried fathers of a child born prior to 1st December 2003 do not have automatic parental responsibility but may obtain it by:

  - Marrying the mother.
  - Having their name registered or re-registered on the birth certificate.
  - Becoming the child's guardian.

- Unmarried fathers of a child born after 1st December 2003 have automatic parental responsibility for their children if they have registered as the father.

- Anyone who has a Residence Order in force in respect of a child he/she is currently looking after.

- Adoptive parents.

- A parent who was not married to the child's mother, but who has acquired PR though a written agreement with the child's mother or through a Court Order.

- A step parent who has formally adopted the children of his spouse where he is not the natural father.

Who does not have parental responsibility?

■ Unmarried fathers of a child born prior to 1st December 2003 who have not taken action as described above.

■ Unmarried fathers of a child born after 1st December 2003 who have not registered as the father or taken action as described above.

■ Grandparents or other relatives.

■ Step parents who have not formally adopted the child.

NB For fathers who do not have PR, but have care of the child, the law accepts that they may 'do what is reasonable in all circumstances of the case for the purpose of safeguarding or promoting the child's welfare'. (S3.5 (a)(b).

Implications for early years settings

Establishing who has PR can be complicated in some families, especially where there have been changes of partner and where either parent has children by more than one partner. It is helpful to focus on who has PR for each child as they register in the setting. Only the parents with PR can register a child in a provision and sign consent forms, including for medical treatment. Children may be collected from the setting by someone who does not have PR with consent of the parent who does.

'Only the parents with PR can register a child in a provision.'

Divorced parents retain equal PR and one parent can only declare that the other must not collect the child if there is a Court Order to substantiate it, in the absence of any amicable agreement between parents.

Where unmarried parents separate, the mother retains PR, but the father only retains PR if he acquired it by the means as above. Again, only a Court Order can decide who may or may not collect a child from the setting where there is no amicable arrangement made between the parents. Where the father did not have PR, the mother may declare that the father cannot collect the child.

Section Two
What needs to be in place in an early years setting

What you need to have in place in a registered early years setting is set out in the statutory welfare requirements of the Early Years Foundation Stage. This is described in Chapter Three.

Settings that are not registrable, such as short term crèches, home visiting projects, family learning and drop in groups, also need to have policies and procedures in place to ensure children are safeguarded and that staff know what to do if they suspect a child is suffering or is likely to suffer significant harm.

Endorsing and implementing the UN convention on the rights of children in early years settings

In this section guidance is offered to settings developing their safeguarding policies and procedures. It also includes guidance on record keeping, confidentiality and information sharing. However, it begins with the recognition of, and commitment to, the rights and entitlements of children.

In the Pre-school Learning Alliance we refer to children's rights and entitlements to be 'strong, resilient and listened to' and this is the fundamental basis of our approach to safeguarding. It is a thread that runs through our safeguarding policy and procedures as well as through the curriculum of the Early Years Foundation Stage.

The Pre-school Learning Alliance supports the 54 Articles contained within the UN convention on the Rights of the Child. The Alliance recognises that these articles apply to children globally and draw attention to the disparity between and within countries and across regions of the world in the way that children receive and enjoy these basic rights. The Alliance supports organisations and statutory agencies to promote the recognition and achievement of children's rights to ensure a better experience for all children.

The following section on children's rights and entitlements sets out what we believe and what all early years services can do to promote these in their day-to-day practice. We believe this is the essential starting point for developing an effective approach to safeguarding children.

Chapter Ten Children's rights and entitlements

Being strong, resilient and listened to

Children in our society are growing up in an increasingly complex world. It is also a world where there seems to be an ever widening gap between rich and poor, the 'haves and the have nots'. Children are the most vulnerable citizens in any society, but where societies are ravaged by extremes of poverty or conflict they are even more vulnerable.

In the first section we discussed ways in which children's rights and entitlements to be strong, resilient and listened to have been not just eroded but completely undermined. This is the essence of child abuse. It is distressing to think of children being treated in ways which frighten and hurt them in ways that have lasting physical and psychological damage.

To grow up psychologically healthy children need to be sure of themselves and confident; they need to be resilient to cope with the normal stresses and strains of life that come their way and they also need to be assured that they have a voice and their views and feelings are heard. Children who have been abused have been denied these sound foundations, but they can be rebuilt, and this is the purpose of remedial interventions with abused children.

Within warm and responsive parenting and within caring child care settings, these principles and their aspects are woven through relationships, care-giving and learning as part and parcel of providing children with the safe nurturing environments they need. Promoting children's right and entitlement to be strong resilient and listened to underpins each of the Every Child Matters five outcomes- to be healthy, stay safe, enjoy and achieve, make a positive contribution and achieve economic well-being. Recognising children's right and entitlement to be strong, resilient and listened to is at the very heart of safeguarding and promoting children's well-being.

'Children are the most vulnerable citizens in any society.'

What it means to promote children's right and entitlement to be 'strong, resilient and listened to'

To be strong means for a child to be:

- secure in their foremost attachment relationships where they are loved and cared for, by at least one person who is able to offer consistent, positive and unconditional regard and who can be relied on;

- safe and valued as individuals in their families and in relationships beyond the family, such as day care or school;

- self-assured and form a positive sense of themselves; including all aspects of their identity and heritage;

- included equally and belong in early years settings and in community life;

- confident in abilities and proud of their achievements;

- progressing optimally in all aspects of their development and learning;

- part of a peer group in which to learn to negotiate, develop social skills and identity as global citizen, respecting the rights of others in a diverse world; and

- participating and be able to represent themselves in aspects of service delivery that affects them as well as aspects of key decisions that affect their lives.

To be resilient means for a child to be:

- sure of their self worth and dignity;

- able to be assertive and state their needs effectively;

- able to overcome difficulties and problems;

- positive in their outlook on life;

- able to cope with challenge and change;

- able to have a sense of justice towards self and others;

- able to develop a sense of responsibility towards self and others; and

- able to represent themselves and others in key decision making processes.

To be listened to means to respect and meet a child's need for adults who are close to them to:

- recognise their need and right to express and communicate their thoughts, feelings and ideas;

- be able to tune in to their verbal, sign and body language in order to understand and interpret what is being expressed and communicated;

- be able to respond appropriately and, when required, act upon their understanding of what children express and communicate; and

- respect children's rights and facilitate children's participation and representation in imaginative and child centred ways in all aspects of children's services.

The intent to promote children's rights and entitlements to be 'strong, resilient and listened to' should span across the breadth of the work of any provision, through the delivery of its services to and relationships with children, families and communities, as enshrined in its policies and ethos, its training, quality improvement and publications.

Chapter Eleven Developing a safeguarding children policy

All settings must have an effective safeguarding policy that states what objectives will be prioritised and what the procedures for doing so will be. Developing a safeguarding children's policy should take account of three main strands of objectives.

1 Being pro-active: This includes what the setting does to ensure children are safe from harm while they are being cared for by people who work in that service.

2 Being reactive: This will include acting on suspicions or concerns about a child who may be suffering or likely to suffer significant harm.

3 Preventative and educative: This will include the information made available to parents and how the care and learning programme fosters children's personal social and emotional development to ensure they are 'strong, resilient and listened to'.

In the Pre-school Learning Alliance, these three strands are referred to as the 'three key commitments'. These commitments provide a basis for the way in which settings can adapt them to relate more closely to their need. The three key commitments are:

1. We are committed to building a *'culture of safety'* in which children are protected from abuse and harm in all areas of our service delivery.

2. We are committed to responding promptly and appropriately to all incidents or concerns of abuse that may occur and to work with statutory agencies in accordance with the procedures that are set down in *What to do if you are worried a child is being abused (HMG 2006)*.

3. We are committed to promoting awareness of child abuse issues throughout our information, learning or advice programmes for adults. We are also committed to empowering young children, through our early childhood curriculum, in promoting their right to be strong, resilient and listened to.

The three key commitments form the strands for the objectives of the policy. These strands need to be expanded to cover all operational aspects.

Key commitment one

We are committed to building a 'culture of safety' in which children are protected from abuse and harm in all areas of our service delivery.

Key commitment one covers:

- Staff to be recruited in line with safe selection and recruitment practices, ensuring all potential employees are fully checked and interviewed for their suitability for the post. This takes account of the need to check identification and qualifications, to ask questions about any unexplained gaps in employment history, to take out verifiable references and to carry out checks with the Criminal Records Bureau (CRB), ensuring practitioners are registered with the Independent Safeguarding Authority (ISA).

- Ensuring there are safe working practices, such as not leaving staff on their own with children or allowing them to take children out on their own - this acts as a safeguard against many risks, including accidents and allegations, not just the potential for child abuse. These may also include how everyday practice such as nappy changing, rest times and toileting take place as well as guidelines for what is appropriate physical contact.

- Safe working practice also concerns how behaviour is managed and how staff respond to children when they themselves are under stress.

- Clear guidelines for staff restricting the use of mobile phones whilst at work and making clear to both staff and parents the purpose of digital video or still cameras, ensuring parental consent is always sought.

- All staff being aware of signs and signals of child abuse and understanding procedures.

- Provision of training for all staff, especially the manager or person acting as the 'designated person' who acts as a co-ordinator on safeguarding for the setting.

- Having a whistle blowing policy that is made known to staff and parents.

'Clear guidelines for staff restricting the use of mobile phones whilst at work.'

Key commitment two

We are committed to responding promptly and appropriately to all incidents or concerns of abuse that may occur and to work with statutory agencies in accordance with the procedures that are set down in *What to do if you are worried a child is being abused (HMG 2006)*

Key commitment two covers:

- The need for clear procedures for recording and reporting concerns to children's social care.

- Following up any initial referral and contributing to any investigation or enquiries made by children's social care, including attending strategy meetings and case conferences.

- Having a complaints procedure that is made known to parents.

- Providing ongoing support to the child and the family in line with the child protection plan.

- Having clear reporting procedures to owners, committees or senior managers in the organisation.

- Having clear protocols for maintaining confidentiality and sharing information appropriately.

Key commitment three

We are committed to promoting awareness of child abuse issues throughout our information, learning or advice programmes for adults. We are also committed to empowering young children, through our early childhood curriculum, in promoting their right to be strong, resilient and listened to.

Key commitment three covers:

- Ensuring information about the setting's safeguarding policy and procedures are available for parents.

- Ensuring information is available for parents about where they can go for help and support.

- Opportunities for parents to discuss with other parents matters to do with parenting that is supportive and informative.

- Planning the early years curriculum to ensure children's personal, social and emotional development promotes their right and entitlement to be strong, resilient and listened to.

Settings can use this guide to developing their own policy. A further example of this is in the Alliance's publication *Policies and Procedures for the Early Years Foundation Stage*. It can also be used as a framework for reviewing existing provision for safeguarding in the setting and for developing good practice.

Chapter Twelve Record keeping and access to records

Recording keeping

In this section, we are not referring to the child's developmental records, which are a shared document between you and the parents. We refer to the personal file that you will have for each child that contains confidential information, such as their registration form, consent forms or other correspondence. This information is confidential and should be kept securely. Where there are child protection concerns and/or actions, you will keep your records in these files, where they cannot be accessed by anyone other than appropriate staff, such as the key person or manager.

Confidential records should NEVER be kept in a separate notebook.

Record keeping is an essential element of child protection. It helps practitioners keep a clear picture of what gave them cause for concern, who they discussed this with and what action they took. No-one can rely on memory or records that are not clear or are inconsistent. Practitioners will need their records for making clear and accurate reports to a strategy meeting or case conference. Records may also be used in a court of law so must meet standards of admissible evidence.

Children's files should be string bound so that papers are not loose, but firmly secured. It is recommended that case notes pages are used. These must always be numbered and placed on the file in order. Records can be filed in either sequence, i.e. in diary formation, with most recent entries last or in reverse formation, with most recent entries on top.

The file should be sectioned out with dividers to provide a section to store registration details and forms, a section for correspondence, a section for contracts and financial information, as well as a section to record notes. Notes on the file are not necessarily about child protection concerns; they could record other matters where something has been discussed or agreed with the parent or where any query has been raised that is over and beyond day-to-day interaction. There should be a confidential section at the back of the file for retaining confidential documents. These for example would include copies of minutes from a case conference or a report on the child from another professional.

Top tips for accurate record keeping are as follows:

1. The name and date of birth of the child should always be clear.

2. The record should have a date of day, month and year as well as relevant entry timing.

3. The name and position of the person making the entry should be clear on every entry.

4. Each entry should be first hand and current wherever possible.

5. The entry should be clear and factual stating exactly what was observed or disclosed and what action was taken.

6. A body map diagram should be used to record any injuries, such as burns, bruises etc.

7. Discussions with parents and decisions taken should be recorded as accurately as possible; entries can be read and signed by parents as accurate.

8. Discussions and decisions made with professionals, whether face to face or by telephone, should be recorded (including times when messages were left).

9. Any witnesses to an event should be noted on the entry and when necessary witness statements should be sought and added to the file.

10. Notes of any meetings attended should be recorded, including any decisions taken that involve an action for the setting.

Parents should be informed that the setting keeps a file for each child and what it contains and why. They should be reassured that it is good practice for the nursery to make notes of important matters as memories cannot be relied on and this way an accurate record is kept. Parents should always be informed if you have a concern, no matter how minor and that you made a note of it. Likewise if they raise a concern, it is helpful that you have made a note of it and that the relevant staff have been informed, for example, a parent might be unhappy that her child's shoes got soaked today or that paint has got on to a new jumper. A note on the file shows you have taken this seriously and that you have taken an action to make sure it does not happen again. This helps resolve very minor complaints and may prevent a matter escalating to a formal complaint level.

Having a note on file that there have been a number of minor concerns helps if you need to feed back to a parent that you have noticed something on a number of occasions and that a matter has now taken on a more serious nature. Similarly if you are completing a referral form, your notes give an accurate history of what has led to the referral being made. Many referrals are made as a result of a number of minor concerns escalating to there being a need to refer; fewer referrals are made as a result of an isolated incident.

Subject or client access to records

Under the Data Protection Act the 'subject' of any manual or computer held records has a right to see the information held on him or her. While it is the child who is the subject of you records, the parent has the right to have access while the child is too young to give informed consent.

Access to records does not mean that the parent has a right to walk into the office and demand to see the file at any time. There may be information on the file that has been provided by another agency and the setting is responsible for maintaining the confidentiality of those 'third parties'.

If a parent wishes to see the content of their child's file they must make their request in writing. You have 14 days to provide the access. At this point you should also seek legal advice as to what is permissible to disclose. You must write to all third parties to request their consent to disclose any information that is concerning them on the file. A third party is anyone named on the file, including all other family members as well as agencies. Where this is refused, this information must be removed from the file. It is usual that other agencies refuse consent to disclose as they would rather the parents went to them directly. When the third party consents or refusals to give consent have been received back the file can be prepared.

Take a photocopy of every document in the entire file. Remove or blank out with a thick pen any third party reference where consent had been refused. Take a photocopy copy of the 'cleaned' file. If a parent is considering legal action, it is advisable to seek legal advice before sharing with the parents directly. This may be best done via solicitors. You can then inform the parents that the file is ready and make an appointment for them to view. It is advisable to go through the file with them and explain the record.

'The parent has the right to have access while the child is too young to give informed consent.'

Example of child protection case notes

Child Protection Case Notes

Name of child: Sarah Lukin   Date of birth: 23.05.07   Page: 1

Date and time	Type of contact	Detail	Action to be taken	Entry made by
11.7.09 9.30am	O&D	Noticed a bruise on the back of Sarah's left thigh when changing her trousers this morning. I said 'Oh dear Sarah, I see you have a bruise. Does it hurt?' Sarah said 'yes it does' Danny done it when I broke his CD'. I asked 'Does Mummy know?' and she said 'Yes'. I replied 'OK, shall I talk to Mummy about it' and Sarah said yes. Reported it to Ann Taylor (manager) Agree to talk to Grace this evening.	Tell the Playleader in charge/manager Talk to Grace (Mum)	Catherine Smith (key person)
11.7.09 4.35pm	PC	Catherine and Ann spoke to Grace and told her what Sarah had said. Anne asked who 'Danny' was - Grace said it was the neighbour's 13 year old son who was looking after her while Grace went to the shop. She said she knew about it and had 'gone mad' when she found out that he had smacked her. Regrets leaving Sarah with Danny and said this would never happen again. Grace spoke to Danny's Mum who is really sorry. Anne explained to Grace that we have a duty to bring this to her attention and make a note of it in the file. It was agreed that Grace seemed to have done the right thing and had taken steps to protect Sarah.	No further action	Ann Taylor (Manager)
29.08.09 11.20am	O&D	I observed Sarah in the home corner with the dolls saying 'Naughty Danny, did Danny hurt you? Danny not to come in'. I went to the home corner and said 'Oh dear, has Danny upset your dolly?' Sarah then told me that Danny had come in the house and was a naughty boy'. I replied Oh I see - shall we talk to Mummy again?'- but Sarah ran off. Later I noticed another bruise on Sarah's left arm as if she had been gripped hard - Told Ann.	Agreed to talk to Grace.	Catherine
29.08.09 4.35pm	PC	Spoke to Grace re above. She was not as helpful as before and said she did not know what Sarah was talking about. Said she would ask her and let us know.	Grace to talk to Sarah and let us know	Ann
01.09.09 9.am	PC	Grace said she had spoken to Sarah and Sarah did not tell her anything, but she said Sarah was fine. Ann said that we were concerned and could not let this go and would have to refer to CSC. Grace was angry and said everything was fine and that if we went to SSD she would take Sarah out of pre-school. Anne said that was her decision, but that we had a duty to report concerns, as was explained in the parent leaflet. Gave reassurance to Grace, but was still not happy	Refer to CSC. Ann and Catherine to complete referral form.	Ann
1.09.09 9.30am	TC	Made referral to SSD using referral form – see attached.	Wait to hear from Social Care Worker.	Ann

Type of contact key:
O&D: Observation/Disclosure; PC: Parent contact; TC: Telephone call; M: Meeting; 3P: Third party; CSC: Children's social care.

Chapter Thirteen Information sharing - confidentiality and when to disclose

Confidentiality and confidential records

What the law says

The Data Protection Act 1998 regulates the handling of information that organisations hold about people on their computers or manual records. This includes how information is obtained, recorded, stored and disclosed.

Information that early years settings hold on families must not be disclosed to anyone else without consent or without good reason under the law. The exception to this is where you:

■ have a concern about a child; or

■ have been asked for information by children's social care or the police.

Sharing information between colleagues in an early years setting is necessary, as staff will need to be aware of critical information in respect of children and families attending. Primarily the information should be between the manager and the key person, but other staff with frequent contact with the child, such as a back-up key person, or who have a managerial responsibility, such as the deputy, should be privy to the information. This sharing of information is acceptable as it is on a 'need to know basis'. It would not be acceptable to share information with anyone outside the setting or with other staff, such as domestic staff, students or staff from another group room.

Confidential information is defined as:

■ personal information of a private or sensitive nature; and

■ which is not already lawfully in the public domain or readily available from another public source; and

■ which has been shared in a relationship where the person giving the information could reasonably expect it would not be shared with others. (*Information Sharing: Guidance for practitioners and managers* HMG 2008)

Practitioners and managers can be said to have a 'confidential relationship' with families. Some families share information about themselves readily; staff need to check whether parents regard this information as confidential or not. Some parents sometimes share information about themselves with other parents as well as staff; the setting cannot be held responsible if information is shared beyond those parents whom the person has 'confided' in. Information shared between parents who take part in organised groupwork is usually bound by a shared agreement that the information is confidential to the group and not discussed outside of it. The setting or group leader is not responsible if that confidentiality is breached by group participants.

Where third parties share information about an individual, practitioners and managers need to check whether it is confidential, both in terms of the subject sharing the information and the person whom the information concerns; for example, if a parent discloses information about another parent, or if another professional shares information informally about a family. Where an early years child care provision is part of a large children's centre, there will need to be rules in place to govern how information is shared between the professionals who work in a multi-agency centre.

Information shared in the context of an early years setting is confidential to the setting and, in some defined circumstances, to the wider organisations. For example, a manager may discuss a family in a supervision meeting with a line manager for the purpose of professional support, clarification and accountability regarding the organisation's procedures. The line manager may share the detail of that information in prescribed circumstances as set out in the procedures.

Here are some examples of confidential and non-confidential information:

Not confidential: 'Mrs Smith discusses with staff and other mothers in the centre quite openly that she is divorcing her husband.'
Confidential: 'Mrs Smith has experienced domestic violence and has confided in the manager and her daughter's key person that she has left her husband and is in a refuge.'

Not confidential: 'Gemma is quite open about the fact that she once misused drugs and makes no attempt to hide old needle scars on her arms.'
Confidential: Gemma confides to her counsellor that she is HIV positive as a result of sharing needles when she used to inject drugs.

Not confidential: 'Ali and Sam now live with their dad.'
Confidential: 'Ali and Sam's mum has severe mental health problems and can no longer look after them, so they now live with their dad.'

Breach of confidentiality

- A breach of confidentiality occurs when confidential information is not authorised by the person who provided it or to whom it relates.

- The impact is that it may put the person in danger or cause embarrassment or pain to that individual.

- It is not a breach of confidentiality if information was provided on the basis that it would be shared with a limited number of people, or where there was consent to the sharing.

The way that confidential information is shared may also present as a breach of confidentiality; if information is shared in such a way that is demeaning to the individual concerned and that does not afford them respect, that is also a breach of confidentiality, as shown in the example below.

Here are a few examples of breaches of confidentiality:

■ 'The staff at the centre are talking in the corridor about where the refuge is and that Mrs Smith and her daughter are there. A neighbour overhears and tells Mr Smith.'

■ 'Gemma's counsellor calls the children's centre about a missed appointment and lets it slip that Gemma is HIV positive. The centre administrator tells the manager who tells the staff.'

■ 'Ali and Sam's key person tells another parent that they live with their dad because "their mum is a bit mental".'

Exceptions to maintaining confidentiality

Confidential information may only be shared without authorisation from the person who provided it or to whom it relates if it is in the public interest. That is to prevent a crime from being committed or intervene where one may have been committed or to prevent harm to a child or adult. Sharing confidential information without consent is done only where not sharing it could be worse than the outcome of having shared it. The decision should never be made as an individual, but with the backup of managers, who can provide support, and sometimes ensure protection, through appropriate structures and procedures. The three critical criteria are:

■ Where there is *evidence* that the child is suffering, or is at risk of suffering, significant harm.

■ Where there is *reasonable cause to believe* that a child may be suffering or at risk of suffering significant harm.

■ To *prevent* significant harm arising to children and young people or serious harm to adults, including the prevention, detection and prosecution of serious crime.

Exceptions to maintaining confidentiality are shown through the following examples:

■ 'The manager alerts social services to the fact that Mrs Smith told another parent that her husband hit the children as well as her, even though she denied it when asked.'

■ 'Gemma's counsellor reports to the police that Gemma has told her that her partner is dealing drugs to young people around the local college and that he carries a gun.'

■ 'Ali and Sam's dad has left the children in the care of another dad who is known to the nursery as a possible sex abuser. The manager reports this to the family's social care worker without letting their dad know first.'

The serious crimes indicated are those that may harm a child or adult; reporting confidential information shared about other crimes such as theft or benefit fraud are not within this remit.

Settings are not obliged to report either suspected benefit fraud or tax evasion committed by clients; however, they are obliged to tell the truth if asked by an investigator. Parents who do confide that they are working 'a little part time job' while claiming should be told this and encouraged to check out their entitlements to benefits as they may be better off declaring earnings than be at risk of prosecution.

Consent

When parents choose an early years setting for their child they will share information about themselves and their families. They have a right to know that information they share will be regarded as confidential as well as be informed about the circumstances, and reasons, when settings are obliged to share information. Parents have a right to be informed that their consent will be sought in most cases, as well as the kinds of circumstances when their consent may not be sought, or their refusal to give consent overridden.

'Parents have a right to be informed that their consent will be sought in most cases.'

Consent must be 'informed', that is the person giving consent needs to understand why information will be shared, what will be shared, who will see information, the purpose of sharing it and the implications for them of sharing that information.

Consent may be explicit or implicit:

- Explicit is obtained specifically at the start of involvement. It may be verbal but preferably in writing. If the proposed sharing is with a different agency or for a different purpose, the consent should be re-sought.

- Implicit consent is implied if the context is such that sharing information is an intrinsic part of the service or has been explained and agreed at the outset.

A setting's policy on information sharing should be explained with parents.

When parents are separated consent to share need only be sought from one parent; this would normally be the parent with whom the child resides. Where there is a dispute, this needs to be considered carefully and legal advice may need to be obtained. Where the child is 'looked after' by the local authority, the local authority is acting as a 'corporate parent' and may also need to be consulted before information is shared.

A child should be able to have the capacity to understand why information is being shared and the implications of that. Therefore for most children under the age of eight in nursery or out of school childcare are not thought to have capacity so consent to share is sought from the parent who has parental responsibility. This is not the same as the need for taking the child's wishes into account. Capacity refers to the mental ability of the child to understand the implications of the information and of the outcome of sharing that.

Decision making and recording for sharing information without consent to disclose

The decision to share information without consent should not be taken lightly. It would be the responsibility of the designated person to do the sharing, but they should discuss this with their line manager first and make sure they have thought through the decision using the following questions and recorded their decision.

The following questions are addressed and recorded in the child's file:

1. Is there a legitimate purpose for sharing the information?

2. Does the information enable a living person to be identified?

3. Is the information confidential?

4. If the information is confidential, do you have consent to share?

5. Is there a statutory duty or court order to share information?

6. If consent is refused, or there good reasons not to seek consent, is there sufficient public interest to share information?

7. If the decision is to share, are you sharing the right information appropriately and securely?

Chapter Fourteen Roles and responsibilities of designated staff in early years settings and organisations

The 'registered person', that is the owner, organisation or management committee of the setting, is responsible for ensuring safeguarding provision meets the EYFS welfare requirements. The larger the organisation the more complex a structure this will be and may need to be overseen by a committee within the organisation with responsibility just for safeguarding.

Every setting will need to have a written document that sets out the role and responsibility of designated people in their organisation, as well as lines of accountability and information sharing; more so in larger organisations where senior managers have an overall responsibility to ensure the child care settings they own and manage are following appropriate procedures and that there is consistency through the organisation.

The designated person

The designated person in an early years setting is usually the manager or deputy. This person should have knowledge and experience of safeguarding matters and be able to support staff with advice, information and training. Their role is to ensure safeguarding procedures are carried out and that staff are supported in raising their concerns and taking appropriate action. The manager/designated person reports all child protection referrals to the designated officer who provides support as well as ensures procedures are being carried out properly.

If a child's key person has concerns they should discuss them with the setting's designated person who will guide them through what needs to be recorded, discussed or not with the parent and what action needs to be taken. The designated person should make the referral and should attend the strategy meeting or case conference. Having the key person attend as well is helpful for the process where the setting can afford for two staff to be off site at the same time.

The designated officer

In most cases a setting manager has to report to someone senior in their organisation, usually a line manager, committee chairperson or owner. This person acts as a designated officer, who carries much of the regulatory responsibility under the welfare requirements to ensure the staff they employ or supervise who manage the day-to-day operation of the setting are competent to do so, especially, in this case, with regard to safeguarding.

The designated officer is responsible for co-ordinating action taken by the setting to safeguard children believed to be at risk of suffering 'significant harm'. This person needs to be kept informed of any child protection investigation or ongoing child protection work that is current. In difficult cases setting managers will need support too and this is a vital part of the supervision of managers. Any investigation resulting in a police criminal investigation and court case is tightly overseen by the designated officer who ensures appropriate legal support is available so that staff acting as witnesses are appropriately prepared.

Sharing confidential information with management committee members needs to be approached with care as committees comprise other parents and there may sometimes be a conflict of interest. Where the chairperson acts as the designated officer, this helps to maintain confidentiality within the management committee structure.

In large organisations senior managers should work together to develop safeguarding strategies for their organisation. Those senior managers with a specific responsibility towards settings may need to be informed about an incident that may have further implications for the organisation. For example, a high profile case that has reached the attention of the press or where they may be allegations made against a staff member. The processes for sharing confidential information to line managers in a setting need to be clear and those acting as designated persons and designated officers should be clear about who they pass information to and how this is to be done in their organisation.

'Sharing confidential information with management committee members must be approached with care.'

The setting manager, senior manager and management committee or owner

Their specific roles include:

- Ensuring that they, and setting staff, are aware of and, where possible, are trained for their safeguarding responsibilities as well as on the child protection associations of social exclusion, drug/alcohol abuse, mental health issues or domestic violence.

- Taking account of diversity and inclusion issues to promote equal treatment of families with a 'child in need' that respect differences in values and traditions, as well as issues of disability and special educational needs.

- Making sure they are familiar with, and keep on premises, the key documents:

  - *What To Do If You Are Worried A Child Is Being Abused* (HMG 2006) (Summary and flow chart poster).
  - *Working Together To Safeguard Children* (HMG 2010).
  - *Framework for the Assessment of Children in Need and Their Families* (DoH 2000).

- Acting in accordance with the setting's child protection procedures when taking appropriate action to safeguard children, including accurate record keeping.

- Ensuring all staff have received safeguarding training within their local authorities within one year of starting employment at the setting.

- Ensuring that through induction, management supervision and in-house training, all staff and volunteers (according to their role) are updated and competent with regard to enacting child protection procedures including:

  - identification of abuse and risk factors;
  - recording concerns ;
  - reporting concerns to managers and to children's social care;
  - acting appropriately with other agencies;
  - carrying out tasks under a child protection plan; and
  - talking to parents about abuse.

- Ensuring staff have access to telephone numbers of their local children's social care teams, including those for other boroughs where there is a child placed in the setting's borough by another borough for housing purposes, but who remains the responsibility or the originating borough.

- Having clear guidelines for volunteers with regard to sharing confidential information.

- Co-operating with police investigations if this arises from a case conference, including ensuring staff who will be court witnesses are briefed on 'Rules of Evidence' by a legal expert.

- Keeping a confidential record of which children have a child protection plan and for which category and discussing these with the designated person at regular intervals in supervision.

- Being alert to when/if high numbers of children have protection plans; the reasons for this to be discussed with children's social care.

- Being aware of the stress involved for staff involved in child protection work and ensuring supervision is offered that deals with their feelings of distress and anger and allows time to debrief. Further support should be provided externally if necessary.

- Ensuring the designated person supports the key person in preparing, or together they prepare, for a strategy meeting or case conference.

Preparing for court

There will be times when child protection strategies do not work and the decision from the investigation is that either criminal charges are to be applied or that children's social care feel that they should apply for a court order to remove a child from parental care. Staff from early years settings, particularly a key person and the designated person, may be called as witnesses, usually by the children's social care department, but sometimes by the parents themselves.

Each case would need to be dealt with as it arises, and prepared for with full legal support. But as a general guide in the event of being called to appear in court as a witness:

■ all staff involved are supported by their designated officer;

■ all staff are fully briefed on Court Rules and Rules of Evidence; and

■ child protection records kept by the staff stand up to scrutiny - that is, they are contemporaneous, (i.e. made at the time of the event happening), are factual, clear and run in date order through the file. Using the templates and following the guidelines given in this publication will achieve this.

Section Three
What to do if you are worried a child is being abused

In this section the child protection process is discussed in more detail to include monitoring the concerns that build up to a referral, making the referral and the role of the early years setting in supporting the child protection process as part of multi-agency working. This section also covers working with parents on child protection matters as well as managing allegations made against staff.

The document entitled *What to do if you are worried a child is being abused* provides a national framework for all agencies working with children to report their concerns and work in partnership to safeguard children effectively.

'..Concerns about a child's welfare can vary greatly in terms of the nature and seriousness of those concerns, how those concerns have been identified and over what duration they have arisen. By ensuring that such concerns are appropriately shared with statutory agencies and other individuals responsible for child protection within agencies, the welfare of children and the safeguards provided for them will be enhanced.'
What to Do If You Are Worried A Child Is Being Abused (HMG 2006) p.1.

This guidance follows this document closely as well as further information contained in *Working Together to Safeguard Children* (HMG 2010).

Chapter Fifteen Procedures for reporting concerns

Recognition of possible abuse and referral

Critical incident

- Managers, staff and volunteers are alert to the signs and signals of child abuse. They understand the implications of drug and alcohol abuse, as well as domestic violence and mental ill health, and the impact this can have on the welfare of young children.

- If the child makes a disclosure of physical, emotional, sexual abuse or neglect, what he/she says is recorded and reported to the manager/designated person immediately.

- If a child shows any visible signs of abuse, such as bruising, burns or injury on any part of the body and it is age appropriate to do so, the key person should ask the child how it happened. For example, "I can see you have a big bruise on your leg. Can you tell me how it happened?" This is recorded immediately. Children are not pushed to respond and are not asked leading questions such as "Did Mummy do it?" or "What else did Daddy do?" Where the child makes a direct disclosure in response, this is discussed with the parent where it is felt that it would not put the child at further risk to do so.

- A member of staff or volunteer may witness an incident between the parent and child that gives cause for concern, for example, involving verbal abuse or aggression. This is brought to the attention of the manager/designated person, and recorded.

- The information is recorded in the child's personal file stating the following:

  - Date and time of the disclosure or when injury or incident was noticed.
  - Verbatim account of what was said by the child and the staff as well as any other adult who was present at the time.
  - Detailed description of any bruising, or other injury, using a body diagram to locate exactly where it was seen.
  - When it was reported to the manager.
  - Signed and dated by the key person or staff member making the entry.

- Each staff/volunteer who witnessed an incident or disclosure should also make a written statement detailing the above for the file.

- The incident is discussed with the parents, unless to do so would put the child at further risk.

- The child's parent's consent for referral to children's social care is sought, but refusal to give consent to refer may be overridden if the manager/designated person and key person agree that this may put the child at further risk.

- Remember, abusers usually know that they are doing wrong and will try to cover up the abuse, for example, by keeping a child at home until a bruise has faded, or threatening a child not to tell.

'Remember, abusers usually know that they are doing wrong.'

Build up of ongoing concerns

- Not all child abuse happens as a critical incident. Often there may be a build up of smaller, seemingly minor concerns, that brought together, build a picture that a child may be suffering, or is likely to suffer, significant harm.

- Each concern that is raised should be recorded in the child's file.

- Always discuss your minor concerns with the child's parents and make a note of their response or anything that you both agree to do, informing the parents that you will be making a note.

- For this reason it is essential to start recording concerns as soon as it appears that something is amiss. If your concerns are justified, a picture will soon emerge in your records and there will be clear evidence.

- If the emerging picture does not suggest a concern about significant harm, but might suggest the child or family might benefit from help, the Common Assessment Framework (CAF) form should be completed with the parent, and the child referred to the appropriate support agency.

- If there now seems to be clear evidence to substantiate a concern about significant harm a referral should be made.

- At any stage, a telephone call can be made to children's social care for advice. They will confirm whether a referral should be made or whether you should continue to monitor and get back to them should you have further concerns.

Referral procedure

- The person acting as the 'designated person' in the setting makes the referral to children's social care providing the following information, which is available on the template referral form in Appendix Two. It is helpful to fill in this form prior to contacting children's social care so that you have all necessary information to hand:

  - Full name of the child, address, date of birth, gender.
  - Name(s) of parents or those with parental responsibility for the child and primary carers if different.
  - Family composition/description of the household, who lives at the child's home, to your knowledge, and names/ages/gender of other siblings and any school or other establishment they attend.
  - Cultural background of the child, languages spoken at home and whether the child has any disability or special need.

- Details of any other agency/professional involved with the child e.g. Health Visitor, GP, Child Development Team.

- Detail of the critical incident that led to the referral- date, time, what was seen/heard and what, if any, action was taken by staff. e.g. discussion with parent, or if the child was taken to hospital.

- Any previous concerns recorded and action taken.

- Any other information that you have on the child's developmental needs, parenting capacity and environmental factors using the Common Assessment Framework triangle as a guide.

Child's developmental needs
Includes information about the child's health; education - learning and progress; emotional and behavioural development; identity; family and social relationships; social presentation (how the child is seen by the outside world); self care skills.

Family and environmental factors
Information about the family's own and wider social context and includes: family history and functioning; wider family; housing; employment; income; family's 'social integration' (how far they are part of the community or how far isolated); community resources.

Parenting capacity
Includes information about the parents' ability to provide for basic care; the child's safety; emotional needs; stimulation; guidance and boundaries; stability.

- Completing the referral form assists social care workers in making a judgement as to whether the concern has met the 'threshold' for a full child protection s47 investigation. It also assists you in thinking about the level of risk a child may be exposed to.

- If you feel you do not know the family well enough to provide information as above, then it is fine not to fill in these sections. Just fill in as much as you can based on what you know.

- Any information provided must be based on factual evidence but where it is your assumption, then that must be clear. What you write in your notes may be used in court as it is admissible evidence. Making judgmental assumptions or statements is inadmissible evidence, and should be avoided, such as "They are a terrible family; everyone says so around here." or being overly positive, such as "They seem so nice, a perfect family. I don't believe anything is seriously wrong".

- Confirm the referral in writing within 48 hours, using the referral form to do so. Alternatively you can use the Common Assessment Framework (CAF) form. This ensures the verbal information given tallies with the information you provide in writing. Keep a copy on the child's file. You should receive a written confirmation from children's social care in response to your written referral within one day. Place this in the child's file immediately. (It is crucial for confidentiality that such documents are not left lying on someone's desk). If you are a group in shared premises, you should agree a safe address for correspondence with the duty children's social care worker.

- If after three days you have not received a confirmation, you should contact children's social care again.

- Any follow up phone call to or from children's social care must be recorded in the child's file, with the data and time, the name of the social care worker and what was said.

- Any further concern must be recorded, such as absence, concerns about how the child presents or behaves, or conversely, any improvement immediately after the critical incident and referral.

- Any further discussion with the parent on the incident or related issue must be recorded on the child's file with the date, time and name of person making the entry.

- It is important that records being built up as a chronological history of events are on proper sheets of paper which are numbered so that they follow in succession. We recommend that you use the 'case record' template for this. You should place a copy in the child's file and use a system where you connect the sheets together rather that have them loosely stored.

Chapter Sixteen What happens after referral?

Being part of the child protection network

The local authority children's social care should decide what action they will take as a result of your referral within one day. This may be to:

- take no further action;

- refer to another agency or provide information or advice;

- carry out an initial assessment; and/or

- take emergency action.

Initial assessment

This is a brief assessment undertaken on a referred child to establish whether:

- this is a child 'in need';

- there is reasonable cause to suspect a child is suffering or is likely to suffer significant harm;

- any services are required and what type; and

- a more detailed core assessment should be undertaken using the *Framework for Assessment of Children in Need and Their Families* (2000) (NB this is not the same as the CAF, but the two are linked together and are based on the same triangle of need).

The initial assessment should be completed within 10 working days. It will focus on the three domains, addressing the following questions, briefly summarised as:

- What are the child's developmental needs; which are currently being met and which are not?

- Are the parents able to respond to these needs and to safeguard the child, promoting their health and development?

- Does the family history and wider environmental factors impact on the parent's capacity to respond to their child's needs and promote their development?

- Is action required to safeguard and promote the welfare of the child and within what timescales?

The initial assessment will involve speaking with the child, the parents and the wider family, as well as gaining information from other professionals who have contact with the child or the family. All of this information will be brought together and then analysed in relation to the family's strengths and weaknesses against vulnerabilities and risk factors, in order to make the right decision for action. Its focus is on the safety and welfare of a child, so if it is felt that concerns about abuse or neglect are not justified, the family may still benefit from support or practical help to promote the child's health and development.

'Focus is on the safety and welfare of a child.'

Where the initial assessment decides a child is 'in need', as defined by s17 of the Children Act 1989, a core assessment may be carried out to determine the types of services that would most benefit the child. A family group conference may be called where this may be discussed openly with the family, reaching an agreement as to what the best course of action should be.

Emergency action

If it is felt that there is risk to a child's life or of serious immediate harm, the local authority children's social care can take emergency action to protect the child and secure their safety. This will follow a strategy meeting between children's social care, the police and other relevant agencies. Legal advice will be sought if it is felt that an Emergency Protection Order is necessary, although, in extreme cases where a child may be in immediate danger, the police can act to remove a child to a safe place while an order is obtained. Sometimes, it may be sufficient and more appropriate in the circumstances to remove a perpetrator from the child's home. After emergency action is taken, children's social care should continue with making s47 enquiries and agree a plan to safeguard the child in the long term. This may or may not involve returning the child home.

Strategy meetings

If it is decided by social care workers that a child is suffering or likely to suffer significant harm, a strategy meeting is convened. This is an initial meeting to discuss and plan an s47 enquiry.

The information provided by early years practitioners is crucial to this process as they see the child and family daily. The meeting is held immediately if the nature of the referral suggests emergency action is needed; otherwise an initial assessment will be made by children's social care, who will then decide whether a strategy meeting is needed. The strategy meeting will comprise children's social care, the police and other agencies as appropriate, including the early years setting as the referrer.

What the early years setting should do at this stage

■ The setting manager/designated person and/or the child's key person will always attend the strategy meeting.

■ Parents are informed that this is to be the case, unless children's social care, for any reason, advises otherwise.

- The referral form is taken along as well as any written update, for example, further issues or concerns, such as absence from the setting, or a general picture of the child since the incident, as well as information about any improvement.

- If it is decided that the child is 'in need', but not suffering or likely to suffer significant harm, the key person and manager/designated person contribute to planning for ensuring the child's welfare and safety. Decisions that are recorded at the meeting will be sent in writing to the setting and are filed immediately in the confidential section of the child's file.

- If it is decided that there are concerns about significant harm, the meeting will decide how the s47 enquiry will take place, whether there is likely to be a criminal investigation and what immediate action should be taken, including initiating a core assessment. The early years setting will always be informed of what will be expected of them at this stage.

The core assessment

If it is decided at the strategy meeting that the initial s47 assessment shows there is risk of 'significant harm', a 'core assessment' will be carried out. This is a more detailed picture of the child's needs and will call upon contributions from appropriate agencies who may have relevant information to share about the child and his or her family. This may include specific assessments from other professionals such as doctors or psychologists. The safety of other siblings in the family will also be taken into account.

The child's wishes and feelings should be ascertained through a one-to-one discussion with a social worker, who may also spend time observing parent and child interactions, especially where a young baby is involved. Specific types of child interviews may take place to gain information about what has happened to them; these may take place without the parent's knowledge in cases where a child may be put in further danger from the parent or alleged perpetrator. These involve highly specialised interviewing techniques designed to engage a child to open up, perhaps using play as a means to encourage communication, but without asking leading questions or causing the child unnecessary distress. Evidence from such interviews may be used in court.

The conclusion of the core assessment may then lead to a case conference if concerns about significant harm appear substantiated; where concerns remain but are not to do with significant harm it may be thought appropriate to offer further support as a 'child in need'. Sometimes concerns about significant harm may be substantiated, but the child may be thought to be no longer at risk of further harm, perhaps because the alleged perpetrator has moved away.

What the early years setting should do at this stage

- The early years setting will be asked to contribute information to this process.

- They may be the referring agency, or where the original referral was about another child in the family, they will be asked to contribute information about the sibling who attends the setting.

- Information may be taken over the phone or through an interview with the children's social care worker.

- Any developmental records are useful to present a summary account of the child's development and well-being. The child's profile book may also provide evidence to gain a wider picture of the child.

- Where no further action is taken at this stage, the setting may be asked to continue to monitor the child and make a new referral if further concerns arise.

Child Protection Case Conference - initial and subsequent

Where the core assessment process substantiates concerns about significant harm an initial case conference is convened where agencies discuss the next course of action. These are always convened by children's social care and are chaired by an experienced senior children's social care manager. They should take place no later than 15 working days after the strategy discussion.

There are a number of strands to their purpose as follows:

- To bring together information from different agencies, discuss and analyse the information from the core assessment about the child's developmental needs and parental capacity to meet them, and ensure the child's safety within the context of the wider family and environment.

- To consider the evidence for whether the child is suffering or likely to suffer significant harm.

- To decide what action to take to safeguard and promote the welfare of the child, including making the child the subject of a child protection plan and what planned developmental outcomes are appropriate and how they will be achieved.

A number of people can make a relevant contribution to a case conference including the child (or representative) family members, social care staff, school or early years staff or others who have had contact with the child such as a health visitor, school nurse paediatrician etc). There may be professionals involved with the parents or other family members, such as those from mental health, substance misuse, domestic violence, learning disability, probation services or GPs. The police from the CAIU will almost always be involved. The conference will follow an agreed agenda that will gather information, analyse it and make recommendations. Information shared and decisions taken, including disagreements, will be minuted.

What the early years setting should do at this stage

■ The key person, in conjunction with the manager/designated person, continues to monitor the child, recording any further concerns or improvements since the initial referral.

■ Any further incident concerning suspicion of significant harm is recorded in the same way and referred immediately to children's social care without waiting for the case conference.

■ At the case conference, written information is prepared using the initial referral and a chronological summary of any further information. Details about the child's attendance over the period in question are helpful, alongside observations about any patterns of non-attendance or reasons given for absences.

■ A summary from the child's developmental records or any specific observations leading to or substantiating concerns should be included. The child's profile is also useful as it gives a rounded picture of the child as an individual, especially when accompanied with photos.

■ The key person and manager/designated person contribute to planning for ensuring the child's development, welfare and safety. Decisions that are recorded at the meeting will be sent in writing to the setting and are filed immediately in the confidential section of the child's file.

■ The key person, in conjunction with the manager/designated person carries out the setting's part in the agreed plan, monitoring and recording outcomes.

■ The setting's manager/designated person keeps the designated officer, i.e. line manager, owner, chair of management committee, informed of any decisions and implications for the setting.

Working with children for whom there is a child protection plan

If the decision of the case conference is that the child has suffered significant harm, or is likely to suffer significant harm in the future, a child protection plan will be drawn up consisting of co-ordinated inputs from appropriate agencies. It will also decide which of the four categories the child is deemed to have suffered, or is likely to suffer, (physical abuse, emotional abuse, sexual abuse or neglect). The named lead social worker will be identified and a core group membership decided. It will also be decided whether legal action needs to be taken at this stage or not.

The child protection plan will be reviewed at least every six months. It should address:

■ Factors associated with significant harm and ways the child can be protected through the inter-agency plan.

■ Short and long term objectives to prevent further harm.

■ Who is responsible for which actions as part of the plan.

■ How the plan will be monitored and evaluated.

■ Who will be responsible for checking that actions have been taken.

A qualified and experienced social worker will be appointed as the lead social worker, or lead professional. He or she will be responsible for developing the protection plan into a more detailed inter-agency plan, as well as ensuring the core assessment is completed and regular contact is made with the child as part of a therapeutic relationship.

The core group is responsible for delivering the child protection plan as a detailed working tool meeting the objectives within the timescales agreed. The core group is usually smaller than the case conference group and less intimidating for the parents. Its first meeting should take place within 10 working days of the case conference with the aim of fleshing out the child protection plan, meeting after that on a regular basis. The lead social worker should ensure meetings and decisions are recorded, updating the child protection plan as necessary.

The child protection plan will address the need to ensure the child's safety, promote his/her health and welfare, and, where in best interests of the child, support the wider family to safeguard the child. There will be specific goals based on what the child's needs are deemed to be and which therapeutic services are required to meet them. It will include when the child must be seen by the lead social worker and set out responsibilities of family members and other professionals, such as heath visitors, GPs, teachers or early years practitioners. It will take account of the wishes and feelings of the child and ensure the parents understand the planned outcomes and are willing to co-operate. Parents will get a copy of the plan as well as members of the core group, such as the early years setting.

What the early years setting should do at this stage

■   The early years setting will be part of the core group of professionals working with children's social care and the family.

■   The key person and/or manager/designated person will attend follow up meetings to specify the role of agencies and allocate specific tasks to carry out as part of the child protection plan.

■   The key person and manager/designated person are clear about their role and tasks, and clarify with the lead social worker if they are not.

■   The role of the key person is very important at this stage in terms of supporting and monitoring the child and talking to the child's parents. They will need supportive supervision from their manager/designated person to ensure they are on track and coping effectively in this task.

■   The key person ensures records of telephone contact with the lead social worker are clearly written and accessible in the child's file.

■   The key person continues to monitor and record progress or otherwise with the plan and records further concerns or critical incidents, using the referral procedure.

■   They participate in the six month child protection review case conferences, contributing follow up information gathered from the notes in the file concerning any discussions with the parents, or further concerns, attendance patterns, as well as material from day-to-day observations and developmental record summaries.

The review case conference

This will be convened to discuss progress of the child protection plan and decide whether the child remains likely to suffer significant harm, and a further child protection plan may be put in place. If it is felt that a child should no longer be the subject of a child protection plan, agencies, including the early years setting, will be informed. A child who is no longer the subject of a child protection plan may still be 'in need' of services for help and support which may include the continuation of an early years placement.

Chapter Seventeen Working with parents in child protection

Effective working relationships with parents

The Early Years Foundation Stage highlights the importance of Positive Relationships as a key theme, and Partnership with Parents as a commitment within this theme. This is to emphasise the continuing primary importance of parents in their child's life with the aim of establishing a relationship of equals.

Effective child protection depends on being able to engage with parents and establish an agreement with the tasks in the child protection plan. Even though parent's wishes and views are taken into account there is not an ethos of working in partnership in the same way as defined in the EYFS. This is because the task of safeguarding a child and promoting their welfare, where significant harm has or may occur, places expectations on the parent as part of legally defined objectives and processes. Local authority children's social care has a legal duty to ensure compliance on the part of parents, otherwise steps may have to be taken to remove children. This cannot be said to be a partnership of equals, although it is still essential that parents are afforded respect and dignity if they are to comply with efforts to make the necessary changes to their parenting or lifestyle, in order to safeguard their children and promote their development and well-being.

'Effective child protection depends on being able to engage with parents.'

When a child who attends an early years setting becomes the subject of a child protection plan it is important that the nature of the relationship as 'partnership' is made clear. It is important that the relationship between the key person especially and the parent is friendly and welcoming as well as accepting and non-judgemental. However, the professional dynamic now involves precise expectations and boundaries, with the responsibilities of the setting made clear. The setting will be required to monitor the child's attendance, development and well-being, as well as record their view of parental capacity and success at engaging with the child protection plan.

The strengths of the input of the early years setting on outcomes for the child lie in the openness of the day-to-day relationship and honesty about what the setting is duty bound to do and why. Staff often have an insight into the strengths of a family and are able to build on this in their interaction with them, but they should not let this cloud their judgement and lead to collusion with, or manipulation by, the parent to undermine the protection process. It is hard to see a parent struggle and, if things go wrong for them, it is tempting to give in to pleas and not let the lead social worker know. Practitioners need sound back up right the way down the line to maintain their priority role in relation to the protection of the child, not the parent.

What the early years setting must do to ensure they work effectively with parents

Managers/designated persons must ensure that they and the key persons work with parents on child protection matters according to the procedures set down. They:

- are clear to parents about their role and why they have to act;

- reassure parents that this is to help them and their child;

- act non-judgementally and transparently;

- are aware of cultural differences, but do not allow cultural assumptions to cloud (deny or increase) their assessment of risk, nor delay them from taking action;

- use interpreters recommended and trained by children's social care if needed;

- meet with the parent and lead social worker after strategy meetings or case conferences to check how the parent is feeling and to go over the setting's part of the plan;

- provide supervision to ensure key persons do not over-identify with the needs of the parent over the needs of the child; and

- use the common assessment framework as a tool to come back to in ensuring that a clear picture with the child at the centre is maintained.

Managers, especially senior managers, owners and chairpersons of management committees, need to take account of the stressful nature of safeguarding work and the impact it can have, especially at the level of the key person. When the initial referral is made there may be threats made to the staff or managers; owners, in particular, can experience threats to their business to try to intimidate them into not taking action. Such behaviour is quite common and often short lived, as once the parents realise that the process is underway and recognise the duty of the setting, they accept that the setting staff are only doing their job. Often it signifies a release for the parents too as many parents are aware that something is wrong and resist seeking help until it finally comes to a head and they have no choice. Settings should be aware too that some threats are real and need to be taken more seriously through reporting them to the police.

While the stresses of safeguarding and child protection cannot be ignored, the rewards of being part of a multi-agency team and having a clear and important role to play are evident when the plan delivers the outcomes intended; early years staff will know the part they played helped the child and family in lasting ways.

Chapter Eighteen Managing allegations against a member of staff

If an allegation of child abuse is made against a member of staff it may come from a parent, another member of staff or from a child's disclosure. It must be reported in the same way as any other child protection referral. The following action should be taken:

- A record must be made of the detail of the disclosure/information that gives cause for concern. This is entered on the file of the child in question.

- The designated officer as line manager, owner or management committee chairperson is informed by the setting manager/designated person.

- Due to the serious nature of the concerns, the disciplinary procedure must be instigated and the member of staff suspended until a full investigation has taken place.

- The relevant sections of the referral form are completed and children's social care is contacted.

- The investigation is carried out by children's social care in the usual way, i.e. first calling a strategy meeting which the setting manager as designated person (unless they are the person against whom the allegation is being made) and the designated officer attend.

- Children's social care and/or the police will continue with the investigation. Managers and staff co-operate fully with the process.

- No further disciplinary action is taken against the member of staff against whom allegations have been made until children's social care have concluded their investigation.

- If it appears from the result of the investigation that the allegations are justified then managers will instigate disciplinary procedures. This must always be done in full consultation with senior managers and with legal advice.

- Where a member of staff is sacked because of a proven or strong likelihood of child abuse, the most senior manager informs the relevant office at the Independent Safeguarding Authority (ISA), for the person's name to be added to the list of people barred from working with children.

It is important to remember that allegations do not always mean that the alleged incident has taken place. The member of staff concerned must be supported and treated with concern and respect. False allegations are very upsetting and stressful and it is important that the staff member is not judged until the result of the investigation is made known.

'Allegations do not always mean that the alleged incident has taken place.'

Whilst the allegations against staff about child abuse seem to be upheld through the investigation, not all cases come to court as there may be insufficient evidence for prosecution. A court can only make a judgement in criminal law where the evidence is 'beyond reasonable doubt'. Evidence in many child abuse cases will not be 'beyond reasonable doubt' but it may meet civil law criteria of being 'on the balance of probabilities'. Where it seems likely that, 'on the balance of probabilities', abuse may well have taken place, then the employer is justified, in law, in dismissing the individual and referring him or her to the ISA barred list.

Appendices

The following template forms are provided:

- Child protection case notes template.

- Child protection referral form.

- Child body diagram.

The template forms are available for purchasers of this publication to download online. Please visit www.pre-school.org.uk/shop/downloads. You will need to log in, or create an account, and enter the access code uht8eag9 . You may use the templates as an exemplar in devising your own.

If you are storing these forms on a computer, it is suggested you only store blank forms, unless your children's records are computerised. Otherwise forms should be completed, printed for storing in the child's file and the completed electronic one deleted if no children's files are electronically stored.

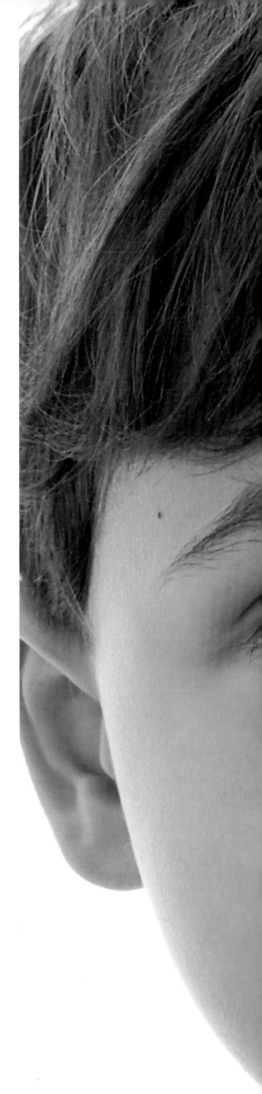

Appendix 1: Child protection case notes template

Child Protection Case Notes

Name of child: Date of birth: Page:

Date and time	Type of contact	Detail	Action to be taken	Entry made by

Type of contact key:
O&D: Observation/Disclosure; PC: Parent contact; TC: Telephone call; M: Meeting; 3P: Third party; CSC: Children's social care.

Appendix 2: **Child protection referral form**

Full name of child:

Date of birth: _____ Gender:

Address:

_____

How long the child has attended the setting?

Patterns of attendance:

Cultural background and languages spoken at home:

Detail of special needs or disability:

Name of parent(s) with parental responsibility at above address:

_____

Name of parent with parental responsibility who is not resident:

Address:

_____ Telephone:

Names of siblings:	Dates of birth:	Gender:	School/pre-school attended:

Name of anyone else living in household:

Relationship to child: _____ Name of significant carers:

Address:

_____ Telephone:

Health Visitor: _____ GP:

Previous Social Worker (if app.) _____ Other agency involved with the child

Detail of the critical incident leading to referral:

```



```

Date: _____ Time:

Was this discussed with the parent? Is the parent aware that the referral is being made? Has the parent given or refused consent to share this information? Give reasons for overriding refusal for consent.

Any previous concerns and action taken. List dates and details:

Child's developmental needs includes general health (including overall growth) and specific health needs, learning and cognitive development and language(s), emotional and behavioural development; identity, family and social relationships, social presentation (how the child is seen by others), self care skills.

Parenting capacity including ability to provide basic care and ensure safety, emotional warmth, stimulation, guidance, boundaries and stability.

Family and environment factors includes family history and functioning, wider family, housing, employment, income, social integration and community resources.

Referred by (manager): _____ Date: _____

Key person: _____

Name of social worker referred to: _____

Telephone number: _____

To receive outcome by (date): _____

90

Appendix 3: **Child body diagram**

Child protection procedure: Child body diagram

Name of child: _____ Date: _____

Make a mark on the diagram where you notice injury/ies

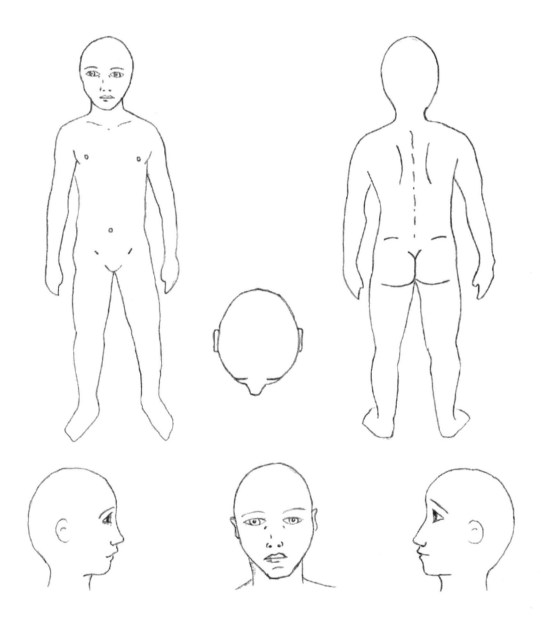

Reading list

Child Protection, Domestic Violence and Parental Substance Misuse: Family experiences and effective practice (2008)
www.dcsf.gov.uk/everychildmatters/_download/?id=2514

Parental Learning Disability and Children's Needs: Family experiences and effective practice (2008)
www.dcsf.gov.uk/everychildmatters/_download/?id=3124

Safeguarding Children and Young People from Sexual Exploitation (2009)
www.dcsf.gov.uk/everychildmatters/_download/?id=6021

Safeguarding Children and Young People who may be Affected by Gang Activity (2010)
www.dcsf.gov.uk/everychildmatters/13537

Safeguarding Children from Abuse Linked to a Belief in Spirit Possession (2007)
www.dcsf.gov.uk/everychildmatters/829

Safeguarding Children in whom Illness is Fabricated or Induced (2008)
www.dcsf.gov.uk/everychildmatters/_download/?id=3161

Safeguarding Children who may have been Trafficked (2007)
www.dcsf.gov.uk/everychildmatters/7290

Safeguarding Disabled Children: Practice guidance (2009)
www.dcsf.gov.uk/everychildmatters/_download/?id=6195

Statutory Guidance on Making Arrangements to Safeguard and Promote the Welfare of Children Under Section 11 of the Children Act 2004 (Updated 2007)
www.dcsf.gov.uk/everychildmatters/1278

UK Border Agency: Statutory duty to safeguard and promote the welfare of children (2009)
www.dcsf.gov.uk/everychildmatters/12870

Vetting and Barring Scheme
www.dcsf.gov.uk/everychildmatters/456

What to Do if you are Worried a Child is Being Abused (2006)
www.dcsf.gov.uk/everychildmatters/926

Information Sharing: Guidance for Practitioners and Managers (2008)
www.dcsf.gov.uk/everychildmatters/resources-and-practice/IG00340/

Working Together to Safeguard Children: A guide to inter-agency working to safeguard and promote the welfare of children (2010)
www.dcsf.gov.uk/everychildmatters/safeguardingandsocialcare/safeguardingchildren/workingtogether/workingtogethertosafeguardchildren/